HARDPRESS.NET
HOME OF HARD-TO-FIND BOOKS

Travels
by Unknown

Address:
HardPress
8345 NW 66TH ST #2561
MIAMI FL 33166-2626
USA
Email: info@hardpress.net

TRAVELS,

&c. &c.

ulated from
[illegible] by

TRAVELS

TO THE WEST OF THE

ALLEGHANY MOUNTAINS,

IN THE STATES OF

Ohio,

KENTUCKY, AND TENNESSEA,

AND BACK TO CHARLESTON, BY THE UPPER CAROLINES;

COMPRISING

The most interesting Details on the present State of

Agriculture,

AND

THE NATURAL PRODUCE OF THOSE COUNTRIES:

TOGETHER WITH

Particulars relative to the Commerce that exists between the above-mentioned States, and those situated East of the Mountains and Low Louisiana,

UNDERTAKEN, IN THE YEAR 1802,

UNDER THE AUSPICES OF

His Excellency M. CHAPTAL, Minister of the Interior,

BY F. A. MICHAUX,

MEMBER OF THE SOCIETY OF NATURAL HISTORY AT PARIS; CORRESPONDENT OF THE AGRICULTURAL SOCIETY IN THE DEPARTMENT OF THE SEINE AND OISE.

SECOND EDITION.

London:

Printed by D. N. SHURY, Berwick Street, Soho;

FOR B. CROSBY AND CO. STATIONERS' COURT;

AND J. F. HUGHES, WIGMORE STREET, CAVENDISH SQUARE.

1805.

CONTENTS.

CHAP. I.

CHAP. II.

CHAP. III.

CHAP. IV.

CHAP. V.

CHAP. VI.

CHAP. VII.

CHAP. VIII.

CHAP. IX.

CHAP. X.

CHAP. XI.

CHAP. XII.

CHAP. XIII.

CHAP. XIV.

CHAP. XV.

CHAP. XVI.

CHAP. XVII.

CHAP. XVIII.

CHAP. XIX.

CHAP. XX.

XXI.

CHAP. XXII.

CHAP. XXIII.

CHAP. XXIV.

CHAP. XXV.

CHAP. XXVI.

CHAP. XXVII.

TRAVELS,

&c. &c.

CHAP. I.

Departure from Bourdeaux.—Arrival at Charleston.—Remarks upon the yellow fever.—A short description of the town of Charleston.—Observations upon several trees, natives of the old continent, reared in a botanic garden near the city.

CHARLESTON, in South Carolina, being the first place of my destination, I went to Bourdeaux as one of the ports of France that trades most with the southern parts of the United States, and where there are most commonly vessels from the different points of North America. I embarked the 24th of

September 1801, on board the John and Francis, commanded by the same captain with whom I returned to Europe several years ago. A fortnight after our departure we were overtaken by a calm, within sight of the Açorian Islands. Saint George's and Graciosa were those nearest to us, where we clearly distinguished a few houses, which appeared built with stone and chalk ; and the rapid declivity of the land divided by hedges, which most likely separated the property of different occupiers. The major part of these islands abound with stupendous mountains, in various directions, and beyond which the summit of Pico, in a pyramidical form rises majestically above the clouds, which were then illumined by the rays of the setting sun. A gentle breeze springing up, we soon lost sight of that charming prospect, and on the 9th of October following entered the Charleston roads, in company with two other vessels which had left Bourdeaux, the one eighteen days, and the other a month before us.

The pleasure that we felt on discovering the shore was very soon abated. The pilot informed us that the yellow fever had made dreadful ravages at Charleston, and was still carrying off a great number of the inhabitants. This intelligence alarmed the passengers, who were fourteen in number, the most of whom had either friends or relatives in the town. Every one was fearful of learning some disastrous news or other. The anchor was no sooner weighed than those who had never been accustomed to warm countries were escorted by their friends to the Isle of Sullivan. This island is situated about seven miles from Charleston. Its dry and parched-up soil is almost bereft of vegetation; but as it is exposed to the breeze of the open sea, the air is generally cool and pleasant. Within these few years, since that bilious and inflammatory disorder, commonly known by the name of the *yellow fever*, shows itself regularly every summer at Charleston, a great number of the inhabitants and planters, who took refuge in the town to escape the intermittent fevers which attack seven-tenths of those resident in the country, have built houses in that island, where they sojourn from the early part of July till the first frost, which usually takes place about the 15th of November. A few of the inhabitants keep boarding-houses, where they receive those who have no settled residence. It has been remarked that foreigners, newly arrived from Europe or the states of North America, and who go immediately to reside in this island, are exempt from the yellow fever.

However powerful these considerations were, they could not induce me to go and pass my time in such a dull and melancholy abode; upon which I refused the advice of my friends, and staid in the town. I had nearly been the victim of my obstinacy, having been, a few days after, attacked with the first symptoms of this dreadful malady, under which I laboured upward of a month.

The yellow fever varies every year according to the intenseness of the heat; at the same time the observation has not yet been forcible enough to point out the characteristic signs by which they can discover whether it will be more or less malignant in the summer. The natives are not so subject to it as foreigners, eight-tenths of whom died the year of my arrival; and whenever the former are attacked with it, it is always in a much less proportion.

It has been observed that during the months of July, August, September, and October, when this disorder is usually most prevalent, the persons who leave Charleston for a few days only, are, on their return to town, much more susceptible of catching it than those who staid at home. The natives of Upper Carolina, two or three hundred miles distant, are as subject to it as foreigners; and those of the environs are not always exempt from it: whence it results that during one third of the year all communications are nearly cut off between the country and town, whither they go but very reluctantly, and seldom or ever sleep there. The supply of provisions at that time is only made by the negroes, who are never subject to the fever. On my return to Charleston in the month of October 1802, from my travels over the western part of the country, I did not meet, on the most populous road, for the space of three hundred miles, a single traveller that was either going to town or returning from it; and in the houses where I stopped there was not a person who conceived his business of that importance to oblige him to go there while the season lasted.

From the 1st of November till the month of May the country affords a picture widely different; every thing resumes new life; trade is re-animated; the suspended communications re-commence; the roads are covered with waggons, bringing from all quarters the produce of the exterior; an immense number of carriages and single-horse chaises roll rapidly along, and keep up a continual correspondence between the city and the neighbouring plantations, where the owners spend the greatest part of the season. In short, the commercial activity renders Charleston just as lively as it is dull and melancholy in the summer.

It is generally thought at Charleston that the yellow fever which rages there, as well as at Savannah, every summer, is analogous to that which breaks out in the colonies, and that it is not contagious: but this opinion is not universally adopted in the northern cities. It is a fact, that whenever the disease is prevalent at New York and Philadelphia, the natives are as apt to contract it as foreigners, and that they remove as soon as they learn that their neighbours are attacked with it. Notwithstanding they have a very valuable advantage that is not to be found at Charleston, which is, that the country places bordering on Philadelphia and New York are pleasant and salubrious; and that at two or three miles' distance the inhabitants are in perfect safety, though even the disorder committed the greatest ravages in the above-mentioned towns.

I took the liberty to make this slight digression, for the informtion of those who might have to go to the southern parts of the United States that it is dangerous to arrive there in the months of July, August, September, and October. I conceived, like many others, that the using of every means necessary to prevent the effervescence of the blood was infallibly a preservative against this disorder; but every year it is proved by experience that those who have pursued that mode of living, which is certainly the best, are not all exempt from sharing the fate of those who confine themselves to any particular kind of regimen.

Charleston is situated at the conflux of the rivers Ashley and Cooper. The spot of ground that it occupies is about a mile in length. From the middle of the principal street the two rivers might be clearly seen, were it not for a public edifice built upon the banks of the Cooper, which intercepts the view. The most populous and commercial part of the town is situated along the Ashley. Several ill-constructed quays project into the river, to facilitate the trading vessels taking in their cargoes. These quays are formed with the trunks of palm trees fixed together, and laid out in squares one above the other. Experience has shown that the trunks of these trees, although of a very spungy nature, lie buried in the water many years without decaying; upon which account they are generally preferred for these purposes to any other kind of wood in the country. The streets of Charleston are extremely wide, but not paved, consequently every time your foot slips from a kind of brick pavement before the doors, you are immerged nearly ancle-deep in sand. The rapid circulation of the carriages, which, proportionately speaking, are far more considerable here in number than in any other part of America, continually grinds this moving sand, and pulverizes it in such a manner, that the most gentle wind fills the shops with it, and renders it very disagreeable to foot passengers. At regular distances pumps supply the inhabitants with water of such a brackish taste, that it is truly astonishing how foreigners can grow used to it. Two-thirds of the houses are built with wood, the rest with brick. According to the last computation, made in 1803, the population, comprising foreigners, amounted to 10,690 whites and 9050 slaves.

Strangers that arrive at Charleston, or at any town in the United States, find no furnished hotels nor rooms to let for their accommodation, no coffee-houses where they can regale themselves. The whole of this is replaced by boarding-houses, where every thing necessary is provided. In Carolina you pay, at these receptacles, from twelve to twenty piastres per week. This enormous sum is by no means proportionate to the price of provisions. For example, beef very seldom exceeds sixpence a pound. Vegetables are dearer there than meat. Independent of the articles of consumption that the country supplies, the port of Charleston is generally full of small vessels from Boston, Newport, New York, and Philadelphia, and from all the little intermediate ports, which are loaded with flour, salt provisions, potatoes, onions, carrots, beet-roots, apples, oats, Indian corn, and hay. Planks and building materials comprize another considerable article of importation; and although these different kinds of produce are brought from three to four hundred leagues, they are not so dear and of a better quality than those of their own growth.

In winter the markets of Charleston are well stocked with live sea-fish, which are brought from the northern part of the United States in vessels so constructed as to keep them in a continual supply of water. The ships engaged in this kind of traffic load, in return, with rice and cottons, the greater part of which is re-exported into Europe, the freight being always higher in the northern than in the southern states. The cotton wool that they keep in the north for their own consumption is more than sufficient to supply the manufactories, being but very few: the overplus is disposed of in the country places, where the women fabricate coarse cottons for the use of their families.

Wood is extravagantly dear at Charleston; it costs from forty to fifty shillings a *cord*, notwithstanding forests, which are almost boundless in extent, begin at six miles, and even at a less distance from the town, and the conveyance of it is facilitated by the two rivers at the conflux of which it is situated; on which account a great number of the inhabitants burn coals that are brought from England.

As soon as I recovered from my illness I left Charleston, and went to reside in a small plantation about ten miles from the town, where my father had formed a botanic garden. It was there he collected and cultivated, with the greatest care, the plants that he found in the long and painful travels that his ardent love for science had urged him to make, almost every year, in the different quarters of America. Ever animated with a desire of serving the country he was in, he conceived that the climate of South Carolina must be favourable to the culture of several useful vegetables of the old continent, and made a memorial of them, which he read to the Agricultural Society at Charleston. A few happy essays confirmed him in his opinion, but his return to Europe did not permit him to continue his former attempts. On my arrival at Carolina I found in this garden a superb collection of trees and plants that had survived almost a total neglect for nearly the space of four years. I likewise found there a great number of trees belonging to the old continent, that my father had planted, some of which were in the most flourishing state. I principally remarked two *ginkgo bilobas*, that had not been planted above seven years, and which were then upward of thirty feet in height; several *sterculia platanifolia*, which had yielded seed upward of six years; in short, more than a hundred and fifty *mimosa illibrissin*, the first plant of which came from Europe about ten inches in diameter. I set several before my return to France, this tree being at that time very much esteemed for its magnificent flowers. The Agricultural Society at Carolina are now in possession of this garden: they intend keeping it in order, and cultivating the useful vegetables belonging to the old continent, which, from the analogy of the climate, promise every success. I employed the remainder of the autumn in making collections of seed, which I sent to Europe; and the winter, in visiting the different parts of Low Carolina, and in reconnoitring the places where, the year following, I might make more abundant harvests, and procure the various sorts that I had not been able to collect during the autumn.

On this account I must observe, that in North America, and perhaps more so than in Europe, there are plants that only inhabit certain places; whence it happens that a botanist, in despite of all his zeal and activity, does not meet with them for years; whilst another, led by a happy chance, finds them in his first excursion. I shall add, in favour of those who wish to travel over the southern part of the United States for botanical researches, that the epoch of the flower season begins in the early part of February; the time for gathering the seeds of herbaceous plants in the month of August; and on the 1st of October for that of forest trees.

CHAP. II.

Departure from Charleston for New York.—A short description of the town.—Botanic excursions in New Jersey.—Remark upon the Quercus tinctoria *or Black Oak, and the nut trees of that country.—Departure from New York for Philadelphia.—Abode.*

IN the spring of the year 1802 I left Charleston to go to New York, where I arrived after a passage of ten days. Trade is so brisk between the northern and southern states, that there is generally an opportunity at Charleston to get into any of the ports of the northern states you wish. Several vessels have rooms, tastefully arranged and commodiously fitted up, for the reception of passengers, who every year go in crowds to reside in the northern part of the United States, during the unhealthy season, and return to Charleston in the month of November following. You pay for the passage from forty to fifty piastres. Its duration varies according to the weather. It is generally about ten days, but it is sometimes prolonged by violent gusts of wind which casually spring up on doubling Cape Hatras.

New York, situated at the conflux of the rivers from the east and north, is much nearer to the sea than Philadelphia. Its harbour being safe, and of an easy access in all seasons, makes it very advantageous to the city, and adds incessantly to its extent, riches, and population. The town consists of more than 50,000 souls, among whom are reckoned but a very small number of negroes. Living is not so dear there as at Charleston ; one may board for eight or ten piastres a week.

During my stay at New York I frequently had an opportunity of seeing Dr. Hosack, who was held in the highest reputation as a professor of botany. He was at that time employed in establishing a botanical garden, where he intended giving a regular course of lectures. This garden is a few miles from the town : the spot of ground is well adapted, especially for plants that require a peculiar aspect or situation. Mr. Hosack is the physician belonging to the hospital and prison, by virtue of which he permitted me to accompany him in one of his visits, and I had by that means an opportunity of seeing those two establishments. The hospital is well situated, the buildings are extensive, the rooms lofty and well aired; but the beds appeared to me very indifferent; they are composed of a very low bedstead, edged with board about four inches wide, and furnished with a mattress, or rather a pallias, filled with oat straw, not very thick, coarse brown linen sheets, and a rug. The prison is remarkable for the decorum, the arrangement, the cleanliness that reigns there, and more especially for the willingness with which the prisoners seem to work at the different employments allotted for them.

Each seemed to be tasked according to his abilities or profession; some were making shoes, and others manufacturing cut-nails. These nails, made by the help of a machine, have no point, and cannot be used for the same purposes as others wrought in the usual way; notwithstanding, a great many people prefer them for nailing on roofs of houses. They pretend that these nails have not the inconvenience of starting out by reason of the weather, as it frequently happens with others; as upon the roofs of old houses a great number of nails may be seen which do not appear to have been driven in more than half or one-third of their length.

During my stay at New York, I took a botanical excursion into New Jersey, by the river side, towards the north. This part of New Jersey is very uneven; the soil is hard and flinty, to judge of it by the grass which I saw in places pulled up. Large rocks, of a chalky nature, as if decayed, appeared even with the ground upon almost all the hills. Notwithstanding, we observed different species of trees; among others, a variety of the red oak, the acorn of which is nearly round; the white oak, *quercus alba*; and, among the different species or varieties of nut trees, the *juglans tomentosa*, or mocker-nut, and the *juglans minima*, or pig-nut. In the low and marshy places, where it is overflowed almost all the year, we found the *juglans-hickery*, or shell-barked hickery; the *quercus prinus aquatica*, which belongs to the series of *prinus*, and is not mentioned in the "*History of Oaks**." The valleys are planted with ash trees, palms, *cornus florida's*, poplars, and *quercus tinctoria's*, known in the country by the name of the black oak.

The *quercus tinctoria* is very common in all the

* The History of Oaks discovered in America by A. Michaux.

northern states; it is likewise found to the west of the Alleghany mountains, but is not so abundant in the low part of Georgia and the two Carolinas. The leaves of the lower branches assume a different form from those of the higher branches; the latter are more sharp and pointed. The plate given in the History of Oaks only represents the leaves of the lower branches, and the shape of them when quite young. Amid these numerous species and varieties of oaks, the leaves of which vary, as to form, according to their age, which generally confounds them with each other; notwithstanding, there are certain characteristic signs by which the *quercus tinctoria* may be always known. In all the other species the stalk, fibres, and leaves themselves are of a lightish green, and towards the autumn their colour grows darker, and changes to a reddish hue; on the contrary, the stalk, fibres and leaves of the black oak are of a yellowish cast, and apparently very dry; again, the yellow grows deeper towards the approach of winter. This remark is sufficient not to mistake them; notwithstanding, there is another still more positive, by which this species may be recognised in winter, when even it has lost its leaves; that is, by the bitter taste of its bark, and the yellow colour which the spittle assumes when chewed. The bark of the *quercus cinerea* has nearly the same property; and, finding this, I made an observation of it to Dr. Bancroft, who was at Charleston in the winter of 1802. Upon the whole, it is impossible to be mistaken concerning these two kinds of oaks; for the latter grows only in the dryest parts of the southern states. It is very rarely more than four inches in diameter, and eighteen feet in height; its leaves are lanceolated: on the other hand, the *quercus tinctoria* grows upwards of eighty feet in height, and its leaves are in several lobes, and very long.

Among the species of acorns that I sent over from the northern states of America to France, and those which I brought with me in the spring of 1803, were some of the black oak, which have come up very abundantly in the nursery at Trianon. Mr. Cels has upwards of a hundred young plants of them in his garden.

The species and variety of nut trees natural to the United States are also extremely numerous, and might be the subject of a useful and interesting monography; but that work would never be precisely accurate provided the different qualities of those trees are not studied in the country itself. I have seen some of those nut trees which, by the leaves and blossom, appeared of the same species, when the shells and nuts seemed to class them differently. I have, on the contrary, seen others where the leaves and blossoms were absolutely different, and the fruit perfectly analagous. It is true there are some, where the fruit and blossom are systematically regular at the same time, but very few. This numerous species of nut trees is not confined to the United States; it is remarked in every part of North America from the northern extremity of the United States as far as Mississipi; that is to say, an extent of more than eight hundred leagues from north to south, and five hundred from east to west. I brought over with me some new nuts of six different species, which have come up exceedingly well, and which appear not to have been yet described.

I left New York the 8th of June 1802, to go to Philadelphia; the distance is about a hundred miles. The stages make this journey some in a day, others in a day and a half; the fare is five piastres each person. At the taverns where the stages stop they pay one piaster for dinner, half one for supper or breakfast, and the same for a bed. The space of ground that separates the two cities is completely cleared, and the farms are contiguous to each other. About nine miles from New York is a place called Newark, a pretty little town situated in New Jersey. The fields that encompass it are planted with apple trees; the cyder that is made there is accounted the best in the United States; however, I conceived it by far inferior to that of Saint Lo, Coutance, or Bayeux. Among the other small towns by the road side, Trenton seemed worthy of attention. Its situation upon the Delaware, the beautiful tract of country that surrounds it, must render it a most delightful place of abode.

Philadelphia is situated upon the Delaware, a hundred miles distant from the sea; at this period the most extensive, the handsomest, and most populous city of the United States. In my opinion, there is not one upon the old continent built upon so regular a plan. The streets cut each other at right angles, and are from forty to fifty feet in breadth, except the middle one, which is twice as broad. The market is built in this street, and is remarkable for its extent and extreme cleanliness; it is in the centre of the town, and occupies nearly one-third of its length. The streets are paved commodiously before the houses with brick; pumps erected on both sides, about fifty yards distant from each other, afford an abundant supply of water; upon the top of each is a brilliant lamp. Several streets are planted with Italian poplars of a most beautiful growth, which makes the houses appear elegantly rural.

The population of Philadelphia is always on the increase; in 1749, there were eleven thousand inhabitants; in 1785, forty thousand; and now the number is computed to be about seventy thousand. The few Negroes that are there are free, the greatest part of whom go out to service. Provisions are not quite so dear at Philadelphia as New York; on which account the boarding houses do not charge more than from six to ten piastres per week. You never meet any poor at Philadelphia, not a creature wearing the aspect of misery in his face; that distressing spectacle, so common in European cities, is unknown in America; love, industry, the want of sufficient hands, the scarcity of workmanship, an active commerce, property, are the direct causes that contend against the introduction of beggary, whether in town or country.

During my stay at Philadelphia, I had an opportunity of seeing the Rev. Dr. Collin, minister of the Swedish church, and president of the Philosophical

Society; Mr. John Vaughan, the secretary; Messrs. Piles, John and William Bortram. These different gentlemen had formerly been particularly acquainted with my father, and I received from them every mark of attention and respect. Mr. Piles has a beautiful cabinet of natural history. The legislature of Pensylvania have presented him with a place to arrange it in; that is the only encouragement he has received. He is continually employed in enriching it by increasing the number of his correspondents in Europe, as well as in the remote parts of the United States; still, except a *bison*, I saw nothing in his collection but what may be found in the Museum at Paris.

The absence of Mr. W. Hamilton deprived me of the pleasure of seeing him; notwithstanding, I went into his magnificent garden, situated upon the borders of the Schuylkill, about four miles from Philadelphia. His collection of exotics is immense, and remarkable for plants from New Holland; all the trees and shrubs of the United States, at least those that could stand the winter at Philadelphia, after being once removed from their native soil; in short, it would be almost impossible to find a more agreeable situation than the residence of Mr. W. Hamilton.

CHAP. III.

Departure from Philadelphia to the Western Country.—Communications by land in the United States.—Arrival at Lancaster.—Description of the town and its environs.—Departure.—Columbia.—Passage from Susquehannah, York, Dover, Carlisle.—Arrival at Shippensburgh.—Remarks upon the state of agriculture during the journey.

THE states of Kentucky, Tennessea, and Ohio comprise that vast extent of country known in America by the name of the Western Country. Almost all the Europeans who have published observations upon the United States, have been pleased to say, according to common report, that this part of the country is very fertile; but they have never entered into the least particulars. It is true that, to reach these new settlements, one is obliged to travel over a considerable tract of uninhabited country, and that these journies are tedious, painful, and afford nothing very interesting to travellers who wish to describe the manners of the people who reside in the town or most populous parts; but as natural history, and more especially vegetable productions, with the state of agriculture, were the chief object of my researches; my business was to avoid the parts most known, in order to visit those which had been less explored; consequently, I resolved to undertake the journey to that remote and almost isolated part of the country. I had nearly two thousand miles to travel over before my return to Charleston, where I was to be absolutely about the beginning of October. My journey had likewise every appearance of being retarded by a thousand common-place obstacles, which is either impossible to foresee, or by any means prevent. These considerations, however, did not stop me; accordingly I fixed my departure from Philadelphia on the 27th of June 1802: I had not the least motive to proceed on slowly, in order to collect observations already confirmed by travellers who had written before me on that subject; this very reason induced me to take the most expeditious means for the purpose of reaching Pittsburgh, situated at the extremity of Ohio; in consequence of which I took the stage * at Philadelphia, that goes to Shippensburgh by Lancaster, York, and Carlisle. Shippensburgh, about one hundred and forty miles from Philadelphia, is the farthest place that the stages go to upon that road.

It is reckoned sixty miles from Philadelphia to Lancaster, where I arrived the same day in the afternoon. The road is kept in good repair by the means of turnpikes, fixed at a regular distance from each other. Nearly the whole of the way the houses are almost close together; every proprietor to his enclosure. Throughout the United States all the land that is cultivated is fenced in, to keep it from the cattle and quadrupeds of every kind that the inhabitants leave the major part of the year in the woods, which in that respect are free. Near towns or villages these

* Till the year 1802, the stages that set out at Philadelphia did not go farther South than to Petersburg in Virginia, which is about three hundred miles from Philadelphia; but in the month of March of that year, a new line of correspondence was formed between the latter city and Charleston. The journey is about a fortnight, the distance fifteen hundred miles, and the fare fifty piastres. There are stages also between Philadelphia, New York, and Boston, as well as between Charleston and Savannah, in Georgia, so that from Boston to Savannah, a distance of twelve hundred miles, persons may travel by the stages.

enclosures are made with posts, fixed in the ground about twelve feet from each other, containing five mortises, at the distance of eight or nine inches, in which are fitted long spars about four or five inches in diameter, similar to the poles used by builders for making scaffolds. The reason of their enclosing thus is principally through economy, as it takes up but very little wood, which is extremely dear in the environs of the Northern cities; but in the interior of the country, and in the Southern states, the enclosures are made with pieces of wood of equal length, placed one above the other, disposed in a zig-zag form, and supported by their extremities, which cross and interlace each other; the enclosures appear to be about seven feet in height. In the lower part of the Carolinas they are made of fir; in the other parts of the country, and throughout the North, they are comprised of oak and walnut-tree; they are said to last about five and twenty years when kept in good repair.

The tract of country we have to cross, before we get to Lancaster, is exceedingly fertile and productive; the fields are covered with wheat, rye, and oats, which is a proof that the soil is better than that between New York and Philadelphia. The inns are very numerous on the road; in almost all of them they speak German. My fellow travellers being continually thirsty, made the stage stop at every inn to drink a glass or two of grog. This beverage, which is generally used in the United States, is a mixture of brandy and water, or rum and water, the proportion of which depends upon the person's taste.

Lancaster is situated in a fertile and well-cultivated plain. The town is built upon a regular plan; the houses, elevated two stories, are all of brick; the two principal streets are paved as at Philadelphia. The population is from four to five thousand inhabitants, almost all of German origin, and various sects; each to his particular church; that of the Roman Catholics is the least numerous. The inhabitants are for the most part armourers, hatters, saddlers, and coopers; the armourers of Lancaster have been long esteemed for the manufacturing of rifle-barrelled guns, the only arms that are used by the inhabitants of the interior part of the country, and the Indian nations that border on the frontiers of the United States.

At Lancaster I formed acquaintance with Mr. Mulhenberg, a Lutheran minister, who, for twenty years past, had applied himself to botany. He shewed me the manuscript concerning a *Flora Lancastriensis.* The number of the species described were upwards of twelve hundred. Mr. Mulhenberg is very communicative, and more than once he expressed to me the pleasure it would give him to be on terms of intimacy with the French botanists; he corresponds regularly with Messrs. Wildenow and Smith. I met at Lancaster Mr. W. Hamilton, whose magnificent garden I had an opportunity of seeing near Philadelphia. This amateur was very intimate with my father; and I can never forget the marks of benevolence that I received from him and Mr. Mulhenberg, as well as the concern they both expressed for the success of the long journey I had undertaken.

On the 27th of June I set out from Lancaster for Shippensburgh. There were only four of us in the stage, which was fitted up to hold twelve passengers. Columbia, situated upon the Susquehannah, is the first town that we arrived at; it is composed of about fifty houses, scattered here and there, and almost all built with wood; at this place ends the turnpike road.

It is not useless to observe here, that in the United States they give often the name of town to a group of seven or eight houses, and that the mode of constructing them is not the same everywhere. At

Philadelphia the houses are built with brick. In the other towns and country places that surround them, the half, and even frequently the whole, is built with wood; but at places within seventy or eighty miles of the sea, in the central and southern states, and again more particularly in those situated to the Westward of the Alleghany Mountains, one third of the inhabitants reside in *log houses*. These dwellings are made with the trunks of trees, from twenty to thirty feet in length, about five inches diameter, placed one upon another, and kept up by notches cut at their extremities. The roof is formed with pieces of similar length to those that compose the body of the house, but not quite so thick, and gradually sloped on each side. Two doors, which often supply the place of windows, are made by sawing away a part of the trunks that form the body of the house; the chimney, always placed at one of the extremities, is likewise made with the trunks of trees of a suitable length; the back of the chimney is made of clay, about six inches thick, which separates the fire from the wooden walls. Notwithstanding this want of precaution, fires very seldom happen in the country places. The space between these trunks of trees is filled up with clay, but so very carelessly, that the light may be seen through in every part; in consequence of which these huts are exceedingly cold in winter, notwithstanding the amazing quantity of wood that is burnt. The doors move upon wooden hinges, and the greater part of them have no locks. In the night time they only push them to, or fasten them with a wooden peg. Four or five days are sufficient for two men to finish one of these houses, in which not a nail is used. Two great beds receive the whole family. It frequently happens that in summer the children sleep upon the ground, in a kind of rug. The floor is raised from one to two feet above the surface of the ground, and boarded. They generally make use of feather beds, or feathers alone, and not mattresses. Sheep being very scarce, the wool is very dear; at the same time they reserve it to make stockings. The clothes belonging to the family are hung up round the room, or suspended upon a long pole.

At Columbia the Susquehannah is nearly a quarter of a mile in breadth. We crossed it in a ferry-boat. At that time it had so little water in it, that we could easily see the bottom. The banks of this river were formed by lofty and majestic hills, and the bosom of it is strewed with little islands, which seem to divide it into several streams. Some of them do not extend above five or six acres at most, and still they are as lofty as the surrounding hills. Their irregularity, and the singular forms that they present, render this situation picturesque and truly remarkable, more especially at that season of the year, when the trees were in full vegetation.

About a mile from Susquehannah I observed an *annona triloba,* the fruit of which is tolerably good, although insipid. When arrived at maturity it is nearly the size of a common egg. According to the testimony of Mr. Mulhenberg this shrub grows in the environs of Philadelphia.

About twelve miles from Columbia is a little town called York, the houses of which are not so straggling as many others, and are principally built with brick. The inhabitants are computed to be upward of eighteen hundred, most of them of German origin, and none speak English. About six miles from York we passed through Dover, composed of twenty or thirty log-houses, erected here and there. The stage stopped at the house of one M'Logan, who keeps a miserable inn fifteen miles from York. That day we travelled only thirty or forty miles.

Inns are very numerous in the United States, and

especially in the little towns; yet almost everywhere, except in the principal towns, they are very bad, notwithstanding rum, brandy, and whiskey * are in plenty. In fact, in houses of the above description all kinds of spirits are considered the most material, as they generally meet with great consumption. Travellers wait in common till the family go to meals. At breakfast they make use of very indifferent tea, and coffee still worse, with small slices of ham fried in the stove, to which they sometimes add eggs and a broiled chicken. At dinner they give a piece of salt beef and roasted fowls, and rum and water as a beverage. In the evening, coffee, tea, and ham. There are always several beds in the rooms where you sleep: seldom do you meet with clean sheets. Fortunate is the traveller who arrives on the day they happen to be changed; although an American would be quite indifferent about it.

Early on the 26th of June we reached Carlisle, situated about fifty-four miles from Lancaster. The town consists of about two hundred houses, a few of them built with brick, but by far the greatest part

* They give the name of whiskey, in the United States, to a sort of brandy made with rye.

with wood. Upon the whole it has a respectable appearance, from a considerable number of large shops and warehouses. These receptacles are supplied from the interior parts of the country with large quantities of jewellery, mercery, spices, &c. The persons who keep those shops purchase and also barter with the country people for the produce of their farms, which they afterwards send off to the sea-port towns for exportation.

From M'Logan's inn to Carlisle the country is barren and mountainous, in consequence of which the houses are not so numerous on the road, being at a distance of two or three miles from each other; and out of the main road they are still more straggling. The white, red, and black oaks, the chesnut, and maple trees are those most common in the forests. Upon the summit of the hills we observed the *quercus banisteri*. From Carlisle to Shippensburgh the country continues mountainous, and is not much inhabited, being also barren and uncultivated.

We found but very few huts upon the road, and those, from their miserable picture, clearly announced that their inhabitants were in but a wretched state; as from every appearance of their approaching harvest it could only afford them a scanty subsistence.

The coach stopped at an inn called the General Washington, at Shippensburgh, kept by one Colonel Ripey, whose character is that of being very obliging to all travellers that may happen to stop at his house on their tour to the western countries. Shippensburgh has scarcely seventy houses in it. The chief of its trade is dealing in corn and flour. When I left this place, a barrel of flour, weighing ninety-six pounds, was worth five piastres.

From Shippensburgh to Pittsburgh the distance is about an hundred and seventy miles. The stages going no farther, a person must either travel the remainder of the road on foot, or purchase horses. There are always some to be disposed of; but the natives, taking advantage of travellers thus situated, make them pay more than double their value; and when you arrive at Pittsburgh, on your return, you can only sell them for one half of what they cost. I could have wished, for the sake of economy, to travel the rest of the way on foot, but from the observations I had heard I was induced to buy a horse, in conjunction with an American officer with whom I came in the stage, and who was also going to Pittsburgh. We agreed to ride alternately.

CHAP. IV.

Departure from Shippensburgh to Strasburgh—Journey over the Blue Ridges—New species of Rhododendrum—*Passage over the river Juniata—Use of the Cones of the* Magnolia Acuminata—*Arrival at Bedford Court House—Excesses to which the Natives of that part of the Country are addicted—Departure from Bedford—Journey over Alleghany Ridge and Laurel Hill—Arrival at West Liberty Town.*

ON the morning of the 30th of June we left Shippensburgh, and arrived at twelve o'clock at Strasburgh, being a distance of ten miles. This town consists of about forty log-houses, and is situated at the foot of the first chain of Blue Ridges. The tract of country you have to cross before you get there, although uneven, is much better; and you have a view of several plantations tolerably well cultivated. After having taken a moment's repose at Strasburgh, we pursued our journey notwithstanding the heat, which was excessive, and ascended the first ridge by an extremely steep and rocky path. We reached the summit after three quarters of an hour's difficult walking, and crossed two other ridges of nearly the same height, and which follow the same direction. These three ridges form two little valleys, the first of which presents several small huts built on the declivity; in the second, which is rather more extensive, is situated a town called Fenetsburgh, composed of about thirty houses, which stand on both sides of the road; the plantations that surround them are about twenty in number, each of which is composed of from two to three hundred acres of woody land, of which, from the scarcity of hands, there are seldom more than a few acres cleared. In this part of Pensylvania every individual is content with cultivating a sufficiency for himself and family; and according as that is more or less numerous the parts so cleared are more or less extensive; whence it follows, that the larger family a man has capable of assisting him, the greater independence he enjoys; this is one of the principal causes of the rapid progress that population makes in the United States.

This day we travelled only six-and twenty miles, and slept at Fort Littleton, about six miles from Strasburgh, at the house of one Colonel Bird, who keeps a good inn. From Shippensburgh the mountains are very flinty, and the soil extremely bad; the trees of an indifferent growth, and particularly the white oak that grows upon the summit, and the *calmia latifolia* on the other parts.

The next day we set out very early in the morning to go to Bedford Court House. From Fort Littleton to the river Juniata we found very few plantations; nothing but a succession of ridges, the spaces between which were filled up with a number of little hills. Being on the summit of one of these lofty ridges, the inequality of this group of mountains, crowned with innumerable woods, and overshadowing the earth, it afforded nearly the same picture that the troubled sea presents after a dreadful storm.

Two miles before you come to the river Juniata, the road is divided into two branches, which meet again at the river side. The right leads across the mountains, and the left, which we took, appeared to have been, and may be still the bed of a deep torrent, the ground being wet and marshy. The banks were covered with the *andromeda, vaccinium,* and more particularly with a species of *rhododendrum,* that bears a flower of the clearest white; the fibres of the stamina are also white, and the leaves more obtuse, and not so large as the *rhododendrum maximum.* This singular variation must of course admit its being classed under a particular species. I discovered this beautiful shrub a second time on the mountains of North Carolina. Its seeds were at that time ripe, and I carried some of them over with me to France, which came up exceedingly well. The river Juniata was not, in that part, above thirty or forty fathoms broad, and in consequence of the tide being very low, we forded it; still, the greatest part of the year people cross it in a ferry-boat. Its banks are lofty and very airy. The *magnolia acuminata* is very common in the environs; it is known in the country by the name of the *cucumber tree.* The inhabitants of the remote parts of Pensylvania, Virginia, and even the western countries, pick the cones when green to infuse in whiskey, which gives it a pleasant bitter. This bitter is very much esteemed in the country as a preventive against intermittent fevers; but I have my doubts whether it would be so generally used if it had the same qualities when mixed with water.

From the crossing of the river Juniata to Bedford Court House, the country, although mountainous, is still better, and more inhabited, than that we travelled over from Shippensburgh. The plantations, although seldom in sight of each other, are near enough to give a more animated appearance to the country. We arrived at Bedford in the dusk of the evening, and took lodgings at an inn, the landlord of which was an acquaintance of the American officer with whom I was travelling. His house was commodious, and elevated one story above the ground floor, which is very rare in that part of the country. The day of our arrival was a day of rejoicing for the country people, who had assembled together in this little town to celebrate the suppression of the tax laid upon the whiskey distilleries; rather an arbitrary tax, that had disaffected the inhabitants of the interior against the late president, Mr. Adams. The public houses, inns, and more especially the one where we lodged, were filled with the lower class of people, who made the most dreadful riot, and committed such horrible excesses, that is almost impossible to form the least idea of. The rooms, stairs, and yard were strewed with drunken men; and those who had still the power of speech uttered nothing but the accents of rage and fury. A passion for spirituous liquors is one of the features that characterise the country people belonging to the interior of the United States. This passion is so strong, that they desert their homes every now and then to get drunk in public houses; in fact, I do not conceive there are ten out of a hundred who have resolution enough to desist from it a moment provided they had it by them, notwithstanding their usual beverage in summer is nothing but water, or sour milk. They care very little for cyder, which they find too weak. Their dislike to this wholesome and pleasant beverage is the more distressing as they might easily procure it at a very trifling expense, for for apple trees of every kind grow to wonderful perfection in this country. This is a remark which I have made towards the east as well as the west of the Alleghany Mountains, where I have known lofty trees spring up from kernels, which bore apples from eight to nine inches in circumference.

At Bedford there are scarce a hundred and twenty houses in the whole, and those but of a miserable appearance, most of them being built of wood. This little town, like all the rest on that road, trades in all kinds of corn, flour, &c. which, with salt provisions, are the only articles they sell for exportation. During the war, in the time of the French revolution, the inhabitants found it more to their advantage to send their corn, &c. to Pittsburgh, there to be sent by the Ohio and Mississippi to New Orleans, or embark them for the Carribbees, than to send them to Philadelphia or Baltimore; notwithstanding it is not computed to be more than two hundred miles from Bedford to Philadelphia, and a hundred and fifty from Bedford to Baltimore, whilst the distance from Bedford to New Orleans is about two thousand two hundred miles; viz. a hundred miles by land to Pittsburgh, and two thousand one hundred miles by water from Pittsburgh to the mouth of the Mississippi. It is evident, according to this calculation, that the navigation of the Ohio and Mississippi is very easy, and by far less expensive, since it compensates for the enormous difference that exists between those two distances. The situation of New Orleans, with respect to the Carribbees, by this rule, gives this town the most signal advantage over all the ports eastward of the United States; and in proportion as the new western states increase in population, New Orleans will become the centre of an immense commerce. Other facts will still rise up to the support of this observation.

On the following day (the 1st of July) we left Bedford very early in the morning. The heat was excessive; the ridges that we had perpetually to climb, and the little mountains that rise between these ridges, rendered the journey extremely difficult; we travelled no more than six-and-twenty miles this day. About four miles from Bedford the road divides into two different directions; we took the left, and stopped to breakfast with a miller who keeps a public house. We found a man there lying upon the ground, wrapt up in a blanket, who on the preceding evening had been bitten by a rattle-snake. The first symptoms that appeared, about an hour after the accident, were violent vomitings, which was succeeded by a raging fever. When I saw him first his leg and thigh were very much swelled, his respiration very laborious, and his countenance turgescent, and similar to that of a person attacked with the hydrophobia whom I had an opportunity of seeing at Charité. I put several questions to him; but he was so absorbed that it was impossible to obtain the least answer from him. I learnt from some persons in the house that immediately after the bite, the juice of certain plants had been applied to the wound, waiting the doctor's arrival, who lived fifteen or twenty miles off. Those who do not die with it are always very sickly, and sensible to the changes of the atmosphere. The plants made use of against the bite are very numerous, and almost all succulent. There are a great many rattle-snakes in these mountainous parts of Pensylvania; we found a great number of them killed upon the road. In the warm and dry season of the year they come out from beneath the rocks, and inhabit those places where there is water.

On that same day we crossed the ridge which takes more particularly the name of Alleghany Ridges. The road we took was extremely rugged, and covered with enormous stones. We attained the summit after two hours painful journey. It is truly astonishing how the vehicles of conveyance pass over so easily, and with so few accidents this multitude of steep hills or ridges, that uninterruptedly follow in succession from Shippensburgh to Pittsburgh, and where the spaces between each are filled up with an infinity of small mountains of a less elevation.

Alleghany Ridge is the most elevated link in Pensylvania; on its summit are two log-houses, very indifferently constructed, about three miles distant from each other, which serve as public houses. These were the only habitations we met with on the road from Bedford; the remaining part of the country is uninhabited. We stopped at the second, kept by one Chatlers, tolerably well supplied with provisions for the country, as they served us up for dinner slices of ham and venison fried on the hearth, with a kind of muffins made of flour, which they baked before the fire upon a little board.

Notwithstanding a very heavy fall of rain, we went to sleep that day at Stanley Town, a small place, which, like all those in that part of Pensylvania, is built upon a hill. It is composed of about fifty houses, the half of which are log-houses; among the rest are a few inns, and two or three shops, supplied from Philadelphia; the distance is about seven miles from Chatler's; the country that separates them is very fertile, and abounds with trees of the highest elevation; those most prevalent in the woods are the white, red, and black oaks, the beech, tulip, and *magnolia acuminata*.

The horse we bought at Shippensburgh, and which

we rode alternately, was very much fatigued, in consequence of which we travelled but very little farther than if we had been on foot; in the mean time the American officer, my companion, was in haste to arrive at Pittsburgh, to be present at the fête of the 4th of July in commemoration of the American independence. In order to gain a day, he hired a horse at Stanley Town, with which we crossed Laurel Hill, a distance of four miles. The direction of this ridge is parallel with those we had left behind us; the woods which cover it are more tufted, and the vegetation appears more lively. The name given to this mountain I have no doubt proceeds from the great quantity of *calmia latifolia,* from eight to ten feet high, which grows exclusively in all the vacant places, and that of the *rhododendrum maximum,* which enamel the borders of the torrents; for the inhabitants call the *rhododendrum* laurel as frequently as the *calmia latifolia.* Some describe the latter shrub by the name of the colico-tree, the leaves of which, they say, are a very subtle poison to sheep, who die almost instantaneously after eating them. At the foot of Laurel Hill begins the valley of Ligonier, in which is situated, about a quarter of a mile from the mountain, West Liberty Town, composed of eighteen or twenty log-houses. The soil of this valley appears extremely fertile. It is very near this place that the French, formerly masters of Canada, built Fort Ligonier, as every part of the United States west of the Alleghany Mountains depended on Canada or Louisiana.

CHAP. V.

Departure from West Liberty Town to go among the Mountains in search of a Shrub supposed to give good Oil, a new Species of Azalea.—*Ligonier Valley.—Coal Mines.—Greensburgh.—Arrival at Pittsburgh.*

ON my journey to Lancaster Mr. W. Lancaster had informed me that at a short distance from West Liberty Town, and near the plantation of Mr. Patrick Archibald, there grew a shrub, the fruit of which he had been told produced excellent oil. Several persons at New York and Philadelphia had heard the same, and entertained a hope that, cultivated largely, it might turn to general advantage. In fact, it would have been a treasure to find a shrub which, to the valuable qualities of the olive-tree, united that of enduring the cold of the most northern countries. Induced by these motives, I left my travelling companion to go amongst the mountains in quest of the shrub. About two miles from West Liberty Town I passed by Probes's Furnace, a foundry established by a Frenchman from Alsace, who manufactures all kinds of vessels in brass and copper; the largest contain about two hundred pints, which are sent into Kentucky and Tennessea, where they use them for the preparation of salt by evaporation; the smaller ones are destined for domestic uses. They directed me at the foundry which road I was to take, notwithstanding I frequently missed my way on account of the roads being more or less cut, which lead to different plantations scattered about the woods; still I met with the greatest civility from the inhabitants, who very obligingly put me in my road, and on the same evening I reached Patrick Archibald's, where I was kindly received after having imparted the subject of my visit. One would think that this man, who has a mill and other valuables of his own, might live in the greatest comfort; yet he resides in a miserable log-house about twenty feet long, subject to the inclemency of the weather. Four large beds, two of which are very low, are placed underneath the others in the day-time, and drawn out of an evening into the middle of the room, receive the whole family, composed of ten persons, and at times strangers, who casually entreat to have a bed. This mode of living, which would announce poverty in Europe, is by no means the sign of it with them; for in an extent of two thousand miles and upward that I have travelled, there is not a single family but has milk, butter, salted or dried meat, and Indian corn generally in the house; the poorest man has always one or more horses, and an inhabitant very rarely goes on foot to see his neighbour.

The day after my arrival I went into the woods, and in my first excursion I found the shrub which was at that moment the object of my researches. I knew it to be the same that my father had discovered fifteen years before in the mountains of South Carolina, and which, in despite of all the attention he bestowed, he could not bring to any perfection in his garden. Mr. W. Hamilton, who had received a few seeds and plants of it from that part of Pensylvania where I then was, had not been more successful. The seeds grow so soon rancid, that in the course of a few days they lose their germinative faculty, and contract an uncommon sharpness. This shrub, which seldom rises above five feet in height is diocal. It grows exclusively on the mountains, and is only found in cool and shady places, and where the soil is very fertile. Its roots, of a citron colour, do not divide, but extend horizontally to a great distance, and give birth to several shoots, which very seldom grow more than eighteen inches high. The roots and the bark rubbed together, produce an unpleasant smell. I commissioned my landlord to gather half a bushel of seed, and send it to Mr. William Hamilton, giving him the necessary precaution to keep it fresh.—On the banks of the creek where Mr. Archibald's mill is erected, and along the rivulets in the environs, grows a species of the azalea, which was then in full blossom. It rises from twelve to fifteen feet. Its flowers, of a beautiful white, and larger than those of the other known species, exhale the most delicious perfume. The *azalea coccinea*, on the contrary, grows on the summit of the mountains, is of a nasturtium colour, and blows two months before.

Ligonier Valley is reckoned very fertile. Wheat, rye, and oats are among its chief productions. Some of the inhabitants plant Indian corn upon the summit of the mountains, but it does not succeed well, the country being too cold. The sun is not seen there for three quarters of an hour after it has risen. They also cultivate hemp and flax, and each gathers a sufficient quantity of it to supply his domestic wants; and as all the women know how to spin and weave, they supply themselves and family, by this means, with linen. The price of land is from one to two piastres an acre. The taxes are very moderate, and no complaints are ever made against them. In this part of the United States, as well as in all mountainous countries, the air is very wholesome. I have seen men there upward of seventy-five years of age, which is very rare in the Atlantic states situated south of Pennsylvania. During my travels in this country the measles were very prevalent. At the invitation of my host I went to see several of his relatives and friends that were attacked with it. I found them all drinking whiskey, to excite perspiration, I advised them a decoction of the leaves of the viscous elm, with the addition of a spoonful of vinegar to a pint, and an ounce of sugar of maple. In consequence of the country being poor, and the population not very numerous, there are but few medical men there; and in cases of necessity they have to go twenty or thirty miles to fetch them.

On the 4th of July I left Archibald's, and posted on toward Greensburgh, which is about eleven miles from it. I had not gone far before I had to cross Chesnut Ridge, a very steep hill, the summit of which, for an extent of two miles, presents nothing but a dry and chalky soil, abounding with oaks and chesnut trees, stunted in their growth: but as I advanced toward Greensburgh the aspect of the country changes, the soil becomes better. The plantations, although surrounded with woods, are not so far apart as in the valley of Ligonier. The houses are much larger, and most of them have two rooms. The land better cultivated, the enclosures better formed, prove clearly it is a German settlement. With them every thing announces ease, the fruit of their assiduity to labour. They assist each other in their harvests, live happy among themselves, always speak German, and preserve, as much as possible, the customs of their ancestors, formerly from Europe. They live much better than the American descendants of the English, Scotch, and Irish. They are not so much addicted to spirituous liquors, and have not that wandering mind which often, for the slightest motive, prompts them to emigrate several hundred miles, in hopes of finding a more fertile soil.

Prior to my arrival at Greensburgh I had an opportunity of remarking several parts of the woods exclusively composed of white oaks, or *quercus alba*, the foliage of which being a lightish green, formed a beautiful contrast with other trees of a deeper colour. About a mile from the town, and on the borders of a tremendous cavity I perceived unequivocal signs of a coal mine. I learnt at Greensburgh and Pittsburgh that this substance was so common and so easy to procure, that many of the inhabitants burnt it from economical motives. Not that there is a scarcity of wood, the whole country being covered with it, but labour is very dear; so that there is not a proprietor who would not consent to sell a cord of wood for half the sum that coals would cost, provided a person would go a mile to fell the trees, and take them home.

Greensburgh contains about a hundred houses. The town is built upon the summit of a hill on the road from Philadelphia to Pittsburgh. The soil of the environs is fertile; the inhabitants, who are of German origin, cultivate wheat, rye, and oats with great success. The flour is exported at Pittsburgh.

I lodged at the Seven Stars with one Erbach, who keeps a good inn. I there fell into company with a traveller who came from the state of Vermont, and through necessity we were obliged to sleep in one room. Without entering into any explanation relative to the intention of our journey, we communicated to each other our remarks upon the country that we had just travelled over. He had been upward of six hundred miles since his departure from his place of residence, and I had been four hundred since I left New York. He proposed accompanying me to Pittsburgh. I observed to him that I was on foot, and gave him my reasons for it, as it is very uncommon in America to travel in that manner, the poorest inhabitant possessing always one, and even several horses.

From Greensburgh to Pittsburgh it is computed to be about thirty-two miles. The road that leads to it is very mountainous. To avoid the heat, and to accelerate my journey, I set out at four in the morning. I had no trouble in getting out of the house, the door being only on the latch. At the inns in small towns, on the contrary, they are extremely careful in locking the stables, as horse-stealers are by no means uncommon in certain parts of the

United States; and this is one of the accidents to which travellers are the most exposed, more especially in the southern states and in the western countries, where they are sometimes obliged to sleep in the woods. It also frequently happens that they steal them from the inhabitants; at the same time nothing is more easy, as the horses are, in one part of the year, turned out in the forests, and in the spring they frequently stray many miles from home; but on the slightest probability of the road the thief has taken, the plundered inhabitant vigorously pursues him, and frequently succeeds in taking him; upon which he confines him in the county prison, or, which is not uncommon, kills him on the spot. In the different states the laws against horse-stealing are very severe, and this severity appears influenced by the great facility the country presents for committing the crime.

I had travelled about fifteen miles when I was overtaken by an American gentleman whom I had met the preceding evening at Greensburgh. Although he was on horseback, he had the politeness to slacken his pace, and I accompanied him to Pittsburgh. This second interview made us more intimately acquainted. He informed me that his intention was to go by the side of the Ohio. Having the same design, I entertained a wish to travel with him, and more so, as he was not an amateur of whiskey, being compelled, by the heat of the weather, frequently to halt at the inns, which are tolerably numerous. I had observed that he drank very little of that liquor in water, and that he gave a preference to sour milk, whenever it could be procured. In that respect he differed from the American officer with whom I had travelled almost all the way from Shippensburgh.

About ten miles from Greensburgh, on the left, is a road that cuts off more than three miles, but which is only passable for persons on foot or on horseback: We took it, and in the course of half an hour perceived the river Monongahela, which we coasted till within a short distance of Pittsburgh. A tremendous shower obliged us to take shelter in a house about a a hundred fathoms from the river. The owner having recognized us to be strangers, informed us that it was on that very spot that the French, in the seven years' war, had completely defeated General Braddock; and he also showed us several trees that are still damaged by the balls.

We reached Pittsburgh at a very early hour, when

I took up my residence with a Frenchman named Marie, who keeps a respectable inn. What pleased me most was my having accomplished my journey, as I began to be fatigued with travelling over so mountainous a country; for during an extent of about a hundred and eighty miles, which I had travelled almost entirely on foot, I do not think I walked fifty fathoms without either ascending or descending.

CHAP. VI.

Description of Pittsburgh.—Commerce of the Town and adjacent Countries with New Orleans—Construction of large Vessels.—Description of the Rivers Monongahela and Alleghany.—Towns situated on their Banks.—Agriculture.—Maple Sugar.

PITTSBURGH is situated at the conflux of the rivers Monongahela and Alleghany, the uniting of which forms the Ohio. The even soil upon which it is built is not more than forty or fifty acres in extent. It is in the form of an angle, the three sides of which are enclosed either by the bed of the two rivers or by stupendous mountains. The houses are principally brick, they are computed to be about four hundred, most of which are built upon the Monongahela; that side is considered the most commercial part of the town. As a great number of the houses are separated from each other by large spaces, the whole surface of the angle is completely taken up. On the summit of the angle the French built Fort Duquesne, which is now entirely destroyed, and nothing more is seen than the vestige of the ditches that surrounded it. This spot affords the most pleasing view, produced by the perspective of the rivers, overshadowed with forests, and especially the Ohio, which flows in a strait line, and, to appearance, loses itself in space.

The air is very salubrious at Pittsburgh and its environs; intermittent fevers are unknown there, although so common in the southern states, neither are they tormented in the summer with musquitoes. A person may subsist there for one-third of what he pays at Philadelphia. Two printing-offices have been long established there, and, for the amusement of the curious, each publish a newspaper weekly.

Pittsburgh has been long considered by the Americans as the key to the western country. Thence the federal forces were marched against the Indians who opposed the former settlement of the Americans in Kentucky, and on the banks of the Ohio. However, now the Indian nations are repulsed to a considerable distance, and reduced to the impossibility of hurting the most remote settlers in the interior of the states; besides, the western country has acquired a great mass of population, insomuch that there is nothing now at Pittsburgh but a feeble garrison, barracked in a fort belonging to the town, on the banks of the river Allighany.

However, though this town has lost its importance as a military post, it has acquired a still greater one in respect to commerce. It serves as a staple for the different sorts of merchandise that Philadelphia and Baltimore send, in the beginning of spring and autumn, for supplying the states of Ohio, Kentucky, and the settlement of Natches.

The conveyance of merchandise from Philadelphia to Pittsburgh is made in large covered waggons, drawn by four horses two a-breast. The price of carrying goods varies according to the season; but in general it does not exceed six piastres the quintal. They reckon it to be three hundred miles from Philadelphia to Pittsburgh, and the carriers generally make it a journey of from twenty to twenty-four days. The price of conveyance would not be so high as it really is, were it not that the waggons frequently return empty; notwithstanding they sometimes bring back, on their return to Philadelphia or

Baltimore, fur skins that come from Illinois or Ginseng, which is very common in that part of Pensylvania.

Pittsburgh is not only the staple of the Philadelphia and Baltimore trade with the western country, but of the numerous settlements that are formed upon the Monongahela and Alleghany. The territorial produce of that part of the country finds an easy and advantageous conveyance by the Ohio and Mississippi. Corn, hams and dried pork are the principal articles sent to New Orleans, whence they are re-exported into the Carribbees. They also export for the consumption of Louisiana, bar-iron, coarse linen, bottles manufactured at Pittsburgh, whiskey, and salt butter. A great part of these provisions come from Redstone, a small commercial town, situated upon the Monongahela, about fifty miles beyond Pittsburgh. All these advantages joined together have, within these ten years, increased tenfold the population and price of articles in the town, and contribute to its improvements, which daily grow more and more rapid.

The major part of the merchants settled at Pittsburgh, or in the environs, are the partners, or else the factors, belonging to the houses at Philadelphia.

Their brokers at New Orleans sell, as much as they can, for ready money; or rather, take in exchange cottons, indigo, raw sugar, the produce of Low Louisiana, which they send off by sea to the houses at Philadelphia and Baltimore, and thus cover their first advances. The bargemen return thus by sea to Philadelphia or Baltimore, whence they go by land to Pittsburgh and the environs, where the major part of them generally reside. Although the passage from New Orleans to one of these two ports is twenty or thirty days, and that they have to take a route by land of three hundred miles to return to Pittsburgh, they prefer this way, being not so difficult as the return by land from New Orleans to Pittsburgh, this last distance being fourteen or fifteen hundred miles. However, when the barges are only destined for Limeston, in Kentucky, or for Cincinnati, in the state of Ohio, the bargemen return by land, and by that means take a route of four or five hundred miles.

The navigation of the Ohio and Mississippi is so much improved of late that they can tell almost to a certainty the distance from Pittsburgh to New Orleans, which they compute to be two thousand one hundred miles. The barges in the spring season usually take forty or fifty days to make the passage, which two or three persons in a *pirogue* * make in five and-twenty days.

What many, perhaps, are ignorant of in Europe is, that they build large vessels on the Ohio, and at the town of Pittsburgh. One of the principal ship yards is upon the Monongahela, about two hundred fathoms beyond the last houses in the town. The timber they make use of is the white oak, or *quercus alba;* the red oak, or *quercus rubra;* the black oak, or *quercus tinctoria;* a kind of nut tree, or *juglans minima;* the Virginia cherry-tree, or *cerasus Virginia;* and a kind of pine, which they use for masting, as well as for the sides of the vessels which require a slighter wood. The whole of this timber being near at hand, the expense of building is not so great as in the ports of the Atlantic states. The cordage is manufactured at Redstone and Lexinton, where there are two extensive rope-walks, which also supply ships with rigging that are built at Marietta and Louisville. On my journey to Pittsburgh in the month of July 1802, there was a three-mast vessel † of two

* An Indian boat.

† I have been informed since my return, that this ship, named the *Pittsburgh*, was arrived at Philadelphia.

hundred and fifty tons, and a smaller one of ninety, which was on the point of being finished. These ships were to go, in the spring following, to New Orleans, loaded with the produce of the country, after having made a passage of two thousand two hundred miles before they got into the ocean. There is no doubt but they can, by the same rule, build ships two hundred leagues beyond the mouth of the Missouri, fifty from that of the river Illinois, and even in the Mississippi, two hundred beyond the place whence these rivers flow; that is to say, six hundred and fifty leagues from the sea; as their bed in the appointed space is as deep as that of the Ohio at Pittsburgh; in consequence of which it must be a wrong conjecture to suppose that the immense tract of country watered by these rivers cannot be populous enough to execute such undertakings. The rapid population of the three new western states, under less favourable circumstances, proves this assertion to be true. Those states, where thirty years ago there was scarcely three hundred inhabitants, are now computed to contain upwards of a hundred thousand; and although the plantations on the roads are scarcely four miles distant from each other, it is very rare to find one, even among the most flourishing, where one cannot with confidence ask the owner, whence he has emigrated; or, according to the trivial manner of the Americans, "What part of the world do you come from?" as if these immense and fertile regions were to be the asylum common to all the inhabitants of the globe. Now if we consider these astonishing and rapid ameliorations, what ideas must we not form of the height of prosperity to which the western country is rising, and of the recent spring that the commerce, population and culture of the country is taking by uniting Louisiana to the American territory.

The river Monongahela derives its source in Virginia, at the foot of Laurel Mountain, which comprises a part of the chain of the Alleghanies; bending its course toward the west, it runs into Pennsylvania, and before it reaches Alleghany it receives in its current the rivers Chéat and Youghiogheny, which proceed from the south west. The territory watered by this river is extremely fertile; and the settlements formed upon the banks are not very far apart. It begins to be navigable at Morgan Town, which is composed of about sixty houses, and is situated upon the right, within a hundred miles of its *embouchure*. Of all the little towns built upon the Monongahela, New Geneva and Redstone have the most active commerce. The former has a glass-house in it, the produce of which is exported chiefly into the western country; the latter has shoe and paper manufactories, several flour mills, and contains about five hundred inhabitants. At this town a great number of those who emigrate from the eastern states embark to go into the west. It is also famous for building large boats, called *Kentucky boats*, used in the Kentucky trade; numbers are also built at Elizabeth Town, situated on the same river, about twenty-three miles from Pittsburgh—the *Monongahela Farmer* was launched there, a sailing vessel of two hundred tons.

Alleghany takes its source fifteen or twenty miles from lake Eria; its current is enlarged by the French Creek, and various small rivers of less importance. The Alleghany begins to be navigable within two hundred miles of Pittsburgh. The banks of this river are fertile; the inhabitants who have formed settlements there export, as well as those of Monongahela, the produce of their culture by the way of the Ohio and Mississippi. On the banks of this river they begin to form a few small towns; among the most considerable are Meadville, situated two hundred and thirty miles from Pittsburgh; Franklin, about two hundred; and Freeport, scarcely one; each of which does not contain above forty or fifty houses.

Let the weather be what it will, the stream of the Alleghany is clear and limpid; that of the Monongahela, on the contrary, grows rather muddy with a few days incessant rain in that part of the Alleghany Mountains where it derives it source.

The sugar-maple is very common in every part of Pennsylvania which the Monongahela and Alleghany water. This tree thrives most in cold, wet, and mountainous countries, and its seed is always more abundant when the winter is most severe. The sugar extracted from it is generally very coarse, and is sold, after having been prepared in loaves of six, eight, and ten pounds each, at the rate of seven-pence per pound. The inhabitants manufacture none but for their own use; the greater part of them drink tea and coffee daily, but they use it just as it has passed the first evaporation, and never take the trouble to refine it, on account of the great waste occasioned by the operation.

CHAP. VII.

Description of the Ohio.—Navigation of that river. —Mr. S. Craft.—The object of his travels.—Remarks upon the State of Vermont.

THE Ohio, formed by the union of the Monongahela and Alleghany rivers, appears to be rather a continuance of the former than the latter, which only happens obliquely at the conflux. The Ohio may be, at Pittsburgh, two hundred fathoms broad. The current of this immense and magnificent river inclines at first north west for about twenty miles, then bends gradually west south west. It follows that direction for about the space of five hundred miles; turns thence south west a hundred and sixty miles; then west two hundred and seventy-five; at length runs into the Mississippi in a south-westerly direction, in the latitude of 36 deg. 46 min. about eleven hundred miles from Pittsburgh, and nearly the same distance from Orleans. This river runs so extremely serpentine, that in going down it, you appear following a track directly opposite to the one you mean to take. Its breadth varies from two hundred to a thousand fathoms. The islands that are met with in its current are very numerous. We counted upward of fifty in the space of three hundred and eighty miles. Some contain but a few acres, and others more than a thousand in length. Their banks are very low, and must be subject to inundations. These islands are a great impediment to the navigation in the summer. The sands that the river drives up form, at the head of some of them, a number of little shoals; and in this season of the year the channel is so narrow from the want of water, that the few boats, even of a middling size, that venture to go down, are frequently run aground, and it is with great difficulty that they are got afloat; notwithstanding which there is at all times a sufficiency of water for a skiff or a canoe. As these little boats are very light when they strike upon the sands, it is very easy to push them off into a deeper part. In consequence of this, it is only in the spring and autumn that the Ohio is navigable, at least as far as Limestone, about a hundred and twenty miles from Pittsburgh. During those two seasons the water rises to such a height, that vessels of three hmndred tons, piloted by men who are acquainted with the river, may go down in the greatest safety. The spring season begins at the end of February, and lasts three months; the autumn begins in October, and only lasts till the first of December: In the mean time these two epochs fall sooner or later, as the winter is more or less rainy, or the rivers are a shorter or a longer time thawing. Again, it so happens, that in the course of the summer heavy and incessant rains fall in the Alheghany Mountains, which suddenly swell the Ohio: at that time persons may go down it with the greatest safety; but such circumstances are not always to be depended on.

The banks of the Ohio are high and solid; its current is free from a thousand obstacles that render the navigation of the Mississippi difficult, and often dangerous, when they have not skilful conductors. On the Ohio persons may travel all night without the smallest danger; instead of which, on the Mississippi prudence requires them to stop every evening, at least from the mouth of the Ohio to Naches, a space of nearly seven hundred and fifty miles.

The rapidity of the Ohio's current is extreme in spring; at the same time in this season there is no necessity for rowing. The excessive swiftness it would give, by that means, to the boat would be more dangerous than useful, by turning it out of the current, and running it upon some island or other, where it might get entangled among a heap of dead trees that are half under water, and from which it would be very difficult to extricate them; for which reason they generally go with the current, which is always strong enough to advance with great celerity, and is always more rapid in the middle of the stream. The amazing rapidity of the Ohio has an influence on the shape of the boats that navigate upon it, and that shape is not calculated to accelerate their progress, but to stem the current of the stream. All the boats or barges, whether those in the Kentucky or Mississippi trade, or those which convey the families that go into the eastern or western states, are built in the same manner. They are of a square form, some longer than others; their sides are raised four feet and a half above the water; their length is from fifteen to fifty feet; the two extremities are square, upon one of which is a kind of awning, under which the passengers shelter themselves when it rains. I was alone upon the banks of the Monongahela, when I perceived, at a distance, five or six of these barges, which were going down the river. I could not conceive what these great square boxes were, which, left to the stream, presented alternately their ends, sides, and even their angles. As they advanced, I heard a confused noise, but without distinguishing any thing, on account of their sides being so very high. However, on ascending the banks of the river, I perceived in these barges several families, carrying with them their horses, cows, poultry, waggons, ploughs, harness, beds, instruments of agriculture, in fine, every thing necessary to cultivate the land, and also for domestic use. These people were abandoning themselves to the mercy of the stream, without knowing the place where they should stop, to exercise their industry, and enjoy peaceably the fruit of their labour under one of the best governments that exists in the world.

I sojourned ten days at Pittsburgh, during which I several times saw the Chevalier Dubac, formerly an officer in the French service, who, obliged, on account of the revolution, to emigrate from France, at first went to settle at Scioto, but very soon after changed his residence, and went to Pittsburgh, where he is now in trade. He has very correct ideas concerning the western country; he is also perfectly acquainted with the navigation of the Ohio and Mississippi, having several times travelled over New Orleans, and gives, with all possible complaisance, to the few of his fellow-countrymen who go into that country, instructions to facilitate their journey, and prevent the accidents that might happen to them.

During my stay at Pittsburgh I formed a most particular acquaintance with my fellow-traveller Mr. Samuel Craft, an inhabitant of the state of Vermont, whom I met, for the first time, at Greensburgh. I learnt of him, among other things, that in this state, and those contiguous to it, the expences occasioned by clearing the land are always covered by the produce of pearl-ashes, extracted from the ashes of trees which they burn; and that there are even persons who undertake to clear it on the sole condition of having the pearl-ashes. This kind of economy, however, does not exist in the other parts of North America; for in all the parts of the east, from New York westward, the trees are burnt at a certain loss. It is true that the inhabitants of New England, which, properly speaking, comprehends all the states east of New York, are acknowledged to be the most enterprising and industrious of all the Americans, especially those who understand domestic economy the best.

Mr. Craft then imparted to me the intent of his journey, which was to be convinced that what he had seen published upon the extraordinary salubrity and fertility of the banks of the river Yazous was correct, and in that case to acquire for himself and a few friends several acres of land, and to go and settle there with two or three families in his neighbourhood who were rather embarrassed. The motive for his emigration to so remote a country was founded, in the first place, on the length of the winters, which in the state of Vermont are as severe as in Canada, and which shackle the activity of its inhabitants more than one third of the year; and in the next place, upon the cheapness of the country's produce; instead of which, in those parts watered by the river Yazous *, the temperature of the climate and the fertility of the soil are favourable to the cultivation of cotton, indigo, and to-

* The river Yazous runs into the Mississippi between the thirty-second and thirty-third degree of latitude.

bacco, the produce of which is a great deal more lucrative than that of the northern part of the United States, and the sale of which is assured by their exportation to New Orleans, where they can go and come by the river in less than a fortnight.

CHAP. VIII.

Departure from Pittsburgh for Kentucky.—Journey by land to Wheeling.—State of agriculture on the route.—West Liberty Town in Virginia.—Wheeling.

MR. CRAFT and I agreed to go together to Kentucky by the Ohio, preferring that way, although longer by a hundred and forty miles, to that by land, which is more expensive. However, as the season of the year being that when the waters are at the lowest, to gain time, and to avoid a considerable winding which the river makes on leaving Pittsburgh, we were advised to embark at Wheeling, a small town situated upon the Ohio, eighty miles lower down the river, but not so far by land. On the 14th of July, in the evening, we set out on foot, and crossed the Monongahela at John's Ferry, situated on the opposite bank, at the bottom of Coal-Hill, a very lofty mountain which borders the river to a vast extent, insomuch that it conceals the view of all the houses at Pittsburgh built on the other side.

After having coasted along the borders of the Ohio about a mile and a half, we entered the wood, and went to sleep at an indifferent inn at Charter Creek, where there was but one bed destined for travellers: whenever it happens that several travellers meet together, the last that arrive sleep on the floor, wrapped in the rug which they always carry with them when they travel into the remote parts of the United States.

The following day we made upwards of twenty miles, and went to lodge with one Patterson. On this route the plantations are two or three miles distant from each other, and more numerous than in the interior of the country, which is a general observation of all travellers. The inhabitants of this part of Pennsylvania are precise in their behaviour, and very religious. We saw, in some places, churches isolated in the woods, and in others, pulpits placed beneath large oaks. Patterson holds a considerable and extensive farm, and a corn-mill built upon a small river. He sends his corn to New Orleans. The rivers and creeks are rather scarce in this part of Virginia, on which account they are obliged to have recourse to mills which they turn by horses; but the flour that comes from them is consumed in the country, not being susceptible of entering into trade. Nobody has ever yet thought of constructing windmills, although there are on the top of several of the hills places sufficiently cleared, that offer favourable situations.

On the 16th of July we arrived at Wheeling, very much fatigued. We were on foot, and the heat was extreme. Our journey was rendered more difficult from the nature of the country, which is covered with hills very close together, to some of which we were almost half an hour before we could reach the summit. About six miles from Patterson's we found the line of demarkation that separates Pennsylvania from Virginia, and cuts the road at right angles. This line is traced by the rubbish that is piled up on lofty eminences, consisting of all the large trees, in a breadth of forty feet. Twelve miles before our arrival at Wheeling we passed by Liberty Town, a small town consisting of about a hundred houses, built upon a hill. The plantations are numerous in the environs, and the soil, although even, is extremely fertile. The produce of the lands vary: they produce from fifteen to twenty bushels of corn per acre, when they are entirely cleared, and only twelve to fifteen when the clearing away is not complete, that is to say, when there are many stumps remaining; for in clearing they begin by cutting the trees within two feet of the ground, and after that dig up the stumps. It is proper to observe that the inhabitants give only one tillage, use no manure, and never let the soil lie idle. The value of this land is according to its quality. The best, in the proportion of twenty to twenty-five acres cleared, for a lot of two or three hundred, is not worth more than three or four piastres per acre. The taxes are from a half-penny to a penny per acre. The hands being very scarce, labour is dear, and by no means in proportion with the price of produce; the result of which is, that in all the middle and southern states, within fifty miles of the sea, each proprietor clears very little more than what he can cultivate with his family, or with the reciprocal aid of some of his neighbours. This is applied more particularly to the western country, where every individual may easily procure land, and is excited to labour by its incomparable fertility.

Within a mile and a half of West Liberty Town the road passes through a narrow valley about four miles long, the borders of which, elevated in many places from twenty-five to thirty feet, present several beds of coal from five to six feet thick, growing horizontally. This substance is extremely common in all that part of Pennsylvania and Virginia; but as the country is nothing but one continued forest, and its population scarce, these mines are of no account. On the other hand, were they situated in the eastern states, where they burn, in the great towns, coals imported from England, their value would be great.

The trees that grow in this valley are very close together, and of large diameter, and their species more varied than in any country I had seen before.

Wheeling, situated on one of the lofty banks of the Ohio, has not been above twelve years in existence: it consists of about seventy houses, built of wood, which, as in all the new towns of the United States, are separated by an interval of several fathoms. This little town is bounded by a long hill, nearly two hundred fathoms high, the base of which is not more than two hundred fathoms from the river. In this space the houses are built, forming but one street, in the middle of which is the main road, which follows the windings of the river for a distance of more than two hundred miles. From fifteen to twenty large shops, well stocked, supply the inhabitants twenty miles round with provisions. This little town also shares in the export trade that is carried on at Pittsburgh with the western country. Numbers of the merchants at Philadelphia prefer sending their goods there, although the journey is a day longer: but this trifling inconvenience is well compensated by the advantage gained in avoiding the long winding which the Ohio makes on leaving Pittsburgh, where the numerous shallows and the slow movement of the stream, in summer time, retard the navigation.

We passed the night at Wheeling with Captain Reymer, who keeps the sign of the Waggon, and takes in boarders at the rate of two piastres a-week. The accommodation, on the whole, is very comfortable, provisions in that part of the country being remarkably cheap. A dozen fowls could be bought for one piastre, and a hundred weight of flour was then only worth a piastre and a half.

CHAP. IX.

Departure from Wheeling for Marietta.—Aspect of the Banks of the Ohio.—Nature of the Forests.—Extraordinary size of several kinds of Trees.

ON the 18th of July in the morning we purchased a canoe, twenty-four feet long, eighteen inches wide, and about as many in depth. These canoes are always made with a single trunk of a tree; the pine and tulip tree are preferred for that purpose, the wood being very soft. These canoes are too narrow to use well with oars, and in shallow water are generally forced along either with a paddle or a staff. Being obliged at times to shorten our journey by leaving the banks of the river, where one is under shade, to get into the current, or to pass from one point to another, and be exposed to the heat of a scorching sun, we covered our canoe a quarter of its length with a piece of cloth thrown upon two hoops. In less than three quarters of an hour we made up our minds to continue our journey by water; notwithstanding we were obliged to defer our departure till the afternoon, to wait for provisions which we might have wanted by the way; as the inhabitants who live in different parts upon the banks of the river are very badly supplied.

We left Wheeling about five in the afternoon, made twelve miles that evening, and went to sleep on the right bank of the Ohio, which forms the boundary of the government, described by the name of the North West territory of the Ohio, and which is now admitted in the union under the denomination of the State of Ohio. Although we had made no more than twelve miles we were exceedingly fatigued, not so much by continually paddling as by remaining constantly seated with our legs extended. Our canoe being very narrow at bottom, obliged us to keep that position; the least motion would have exposed us to being overset. However, in the course of a few days custom made these inconveniences disappear, and we attained the art of travelling comfortably.

We took three days and a half in going to Marietta, about a hundred miles from Wheeling. Our second day was thirty miles, the third forty, and on the fourth in the morning we reached this little town, situated at the mouth of the great Muskingum. The first day, wholly taken up with this mode of travelling, so novel to us, and which did not appear to me to be very safe, I did not bend my attention further; but on the following day, better used to this kind of navigation, I observed more tranquilly from our canoe, the aspect that the borders of this magnificent river presented.

Leaving Pittsburgh, the Ohio flows between two ridges, or lofty mountains, nearly of the same height, which we judged to be about two hundred fathoms. Frequently they appeared undulated at their summit, at other times it seemed as though they had been completely level. These hills continue uninterruptedly for the space of a mile or more, then a slight interval is observed, that sometimes affords a passage to the rivers that empty themselves into the Ohio; but most commonly another hill of the same height begins at a very short distance from the place where the preceding one left off. These mountains rise successively for the space of three hundred miles, and from our canoe we were enabled to observe them more distinctly, as they were more or less distant from the borders of the river. Their direction is parallel to the chain of the Alleghanies; and although they are at times from forty to a hundred miles distant from them, and that for an extent of two hundred miles, one cannot help looking upon them as belonging to these mountains. All that part of Virginia situated upon the left bank of the Ohio is excessively mountainous, covered with forests, and almost uninhabited; where I have been told by those who live on the banks of the Ohio, they go every winter to hunt bears.

They give the name of river-bottoms and flat-bottoms to the flat and woody ground between the foot of these mountains and the banks of the river, the space of which is sometimes five or six miles broad. The major part of the rivers which empty themselves into the Ohio have also these river-bottoms, which, as well as those in question, are of an easy culture, but nothing equal to the fertility of the banks of the Ohio. The soil is a true vegetable *humus*, produced by the thick bed of leaves with which the earth is loaded every year, and which is speedily converted into mould by the humidity that reigns in these forests. But what adds still more to the thickness of these successive beds of vegetable earth are the trunks of enormous trees, thrown down by time, with which the surface of the soil is bestrewed in every part, and which rapidly decays. In more than a thousand leagues of the country, over which I have travelled at different epochs, in North America, I do not remember having seen one to compare with the latter for the vegetative strength of the forests. The best sort of land in Kentucky and Tenessea, situated beyond the mountains of Cumberland, is much the same; but the trees do not grow to such a size as on the borders of the Ohio. Thirty-six miles before our arrival at Marietta we stopped at the hut of one of the inhabitants of the right bank, who shewed us, about fifty yards from his door, a palm-tree, or *platanus occidentalis*, the trunk of which was swelled to an amazing size; we measured it four feet beyond the surface of the soil, and found it forty-seven feet in circumference. It appeared to keep the same dimensions for the height of fifteen or twenty feet, it then divided into several branches of a proportionate size. By its external appearance no one could tell that the tree was hollow; however I assured myself it was by striking it in several places with a billet. Our host told us that if we would spend the day with him he would shew us others as large, in several parts of the wood, within two or three miles of the river. This circumstance supports the observations which my father made, when travelling in that part of the country, that the poplar and palm are, of all the trees in North America, those that attain the greatest diameter.

" About fifteen miles," said he, " up the river " Muskingum, in a small island of the Ohio, we " found a palm-tree, or *platanus occidentalis*, the " circumference of which, five feet from the surface " of the earth, where the trunk was most uniform, " was forty feet four inches, which makes about " thirteen feet in diameter. Twenty years prior to " my travels, General Washington had measured " this same tree, and had found it nearly of the " same dimensions. I have also measured palms in " Kentucky, but I never met with any above fifteen " or sixteen feet in circumference. These trees " generally grow in marshy places.

" The largest tree in North America, after the " palm, is the poplar, or *liriodendron tulipifera*. " Its circumference is sometimes fifteen, sixteen, " and even eighteen feet: Kentucky is their native " country; between Beard Town and Louisville we

" saw several parts of the wood which were exclu-
" sively composed of them. The soil is clayey,
" cold and marshy; but never inundated.

" The trees that are usually found in the forests
" that border the Ohio are the palm, or *platanus*
" *occidentalis;* the poplar, the beach-tree, the *mag-*
" *nolia acuminata*, the *celtis occidentalis*, the acacia,
" the sugar-maple, the red maple, the *populus nigra*,
" and several species of nut-trees; the most com-
" mon shrubs are, the *annona triloba*, the *evonimus*
" *latifolius*, and the *laurus bensoin*."

CHAP. X.

Marietta.—Ship building.—Departure for Gallipoli.—Falling in with a Kentucky Boat.—Point-Pleasant.—The Great Kenhaway.

MARIETTA, the chief of the settlements on the New Continent, is situated upon the right bank of the Great Muskingum, at its *embouchure* in the Ohio. This town, which fifteen years ago was not in existence, is now composed of more than two hundred houses, some of which are built of brick, but the greatest part of wood. There are several from two to three stories high, which are somewhat elegantly built; nearly all of them are in front of the Ohio. The mountains which from Pittsburgh run by the side of this river, are at Marietta some distance from its banks, and leave a considerable extent of even ground, which will facilitate, in every respect, the enlarging of the town upon a regular plan, and afford its inhabitants the most advantageous and agreeable situations; it will not be attended with the inconveniences that are met with at Pittsburgh, which is locked in on all sides by lofty mountains.

The inhabitants of Marietta were the first that had an idea of exporting directly to the Carribbee Islands the produce of the country, in a vessel built in their own town, which they sent to Jamaica. The success which crowned this first attempt excited such emulation among the inhabitants of that part of the Western Country, that several new vessels were launched at Pittsburgh and Louisville, and expedited to the isles, or to New York and Philadelphia. The ship yard at Marietta is situated near the town, on the Great Muskingum. When I was there they were building three brigs, one of which was of two hundred and twenty tons burthen.

The river Muskingum takes its source toward Lake Eria; it is not navigable for two hundred miles from its mouth in the Ohio, where it is about a hundred and sixty fathoms broad. The country that it runs through, and especially its banks, are extremely fertile.

Near the town of Marietta are the remains of several Indian fortifications. When they were discovered, they were full of trees of the same nature as those of the neighbouring forests, some of which were upwards of three feet diameter. These trees have been hewn down, and the ground is now almost entirely cultivated with Indian corn.

Major-General Hart, with whose son I was acquainted at Marietta, gave, in the Columbia Magazine for the year 1787, Vol. I. No. 9, a plan and a minute description of these ancient fortifications of the Indians: the translation of which is given in his Travels in Upper Pennsylvania. This officer, of the most distinguished merit, fell in the famous battle that General St. Clair lost in 1791, near Lake Eria, against the united savages. When I was at Marietta, General St. Clair was Governor of the State of Ohio, a post which he occupied till this state was admitted in the union. His Excellency coming from Pittsburgh and going to Chillicotha, alighted at the inn where I lodged. As he was travelling in an old chaise, and without a servant, he did not at first attract my attention. In the United States, those who are called by the wish of their fellow-citizens to exercise these important functions do not change their dress, continue dwelling in their own houses, and live like private individuals, without showing more ostentation, or incurring more expense. The emoluments attached to this office varies in every state; that of South Carolina, one of the richest of the union, gives its governor 4280 piastres, while the Governor of Kentucky receives no more than twelve or fifteen hundred. The inhabitants of the State of Ohio are divided in opinion concerning the political conduct of General St. Clair. With respect to talents, he has the reputation of being a better lawyer than a soldier.

On the eve of my departure I met a Frenchman at Marietta, who is settled on the banks of the Great Muskingum, about twenty miles from the town. I regretted much my inability to accept the invitation that he gave me to go and see him at his plantation, which would have given me time to make more extensive observations in that part of the Western Country.

On the 21st of July we set out from Marietta for Gallipoli, which is a distance of about a hundred miles. We reached there after having been four days on the water. The inhabitants of the country, by putting off from the shore in the night time, would have made that passage in two days and a half or three days. According to the calculation that we made, the mean force of the stream was about a mile and a half an hour; it is hardly to be perceived in those parts where the water is very deep; but as you get nearer the isles, which, as I have said before, are very numerous, the bed of the river diminishes in depth, so that frequently there is not a foot of water out of the main channel. Whenever we came near those shallows the swiftness of the current was extreme, and the canoe was carried away like an arrow, which led us to observe that it was only as we distanced the islands that the bed increases in depth, and that the stream becomes less rapid.

On the day of our departure we joined, in the evening, a Kentucky boat, destined for Cincinnati. This boat, about forty feet long and fifteen broad, was loaded with bar iron and brass pots. There was also an emigrant family in it, consisting of the father, mother, and seven children, with all their furniture and implements of husbandry. The boatmen, three in number, granted us, without difficulty, permission to fasten our canoe to the end of their boat, and to pass the night with them. We intended, by that means, to accelerate our journey, by not putting up at night, as we had before been accustomed to do, and hoped to spend a more comfortable night than the preceding one, during which we had been sadly tormented by the fleas, with which the greater part of the houses where we had slept, from the moment of our embarkation, had been infested. However our hopes were frustrated; for so far from being comfortable, we were still more incommoded. In the course of my travels it was only on the banks of the Ohio that I experienced this inconvenience.

We were on the point of leaving them about two in the morning, when the boat ran aground. Under these circumstances we could not desert our hosts, who had entertained us with their best, and who had made us partake of a wild turkey which they had shot the preceding evening on the banks of the river. We got into the water with the boatmen, and by the help of large sticks that we made use of as oars succeeded in pushing the vessel afloat, after two hours' painful efforts.

In the course of the night we passed the mouth of the Little Kenhaway, which, after having watered that part of Virginia, empties itself into the Ohio, on its right bank. Its borders are not inhabited for more than fifteen or twenty miles from its *embou-*

chure. The remainder of the country is so mountainous that they will not think of forming settlements there this long time. About five miles on this side the mouth of this little river, and on the right bank of the Ohio, is situated Bellepree, where there are not more than a dozen houses; but the settlements formed in the environs increase rapidly. This intelligence was given us at a house where we stopped after having left the Kentucky boat.

On the 23d of July, about ten in the morning, we discovered Point Pleasant, situated a little above the mouth of the Great Kenhaway, at the extremity of a point formed by the right bank of this river, which runs nearly in a direct line as far as the middle of the Ohio. What makes the situation more beautiful is, that for four or five miles on this side the Point, the Ohio, four hundred fathoms broad, continues the same breadth the whole of that extent, and presents on every side the most perfect line. Its borders, sloping, and elevated from twenty-five to forty feet, are, as in the whole of its windings, planted, at their base, with willows from fifteen to eighteen feet in height, the drooping branches and foliage of which form a pleasing contrast to the sugar maples, red maples, and ash trees, situated immediately above. The latter, in return, are overlooked by palms, poplars, beeches, magnolias of the highest elevation, the enormous branches of which, attracted by a more splendid light and easier expansion, extend toward the borders, overshadowing the river, at the same time completely covering the trees situated under them. This natural display, which reigns upon the two banks, affords on each side a regular arch, the shadow of which, reflected by the crystal stream, embellishes, in an extraordinary degree, this magnificent *coup d'œil.*

The Ohio at Marietta presents a perspective somewhat similar, perhaps even more picturesque than the one I have just described, through the houses of this little town, that we perceived five or six miles off, the situation of which is fronting the middle of the river, going up.

The Great Kenhaway, more known in the country under that denomination than by that of the New River, which it bears in some charts, takes its source at the foot of the Yellow Mountain in Tennessea, but the mass of its waters proceed from one part of the Alleghany Mountains. The falls and currents that are so frequently met with in this river, for upward of four hundred miles, will always be an obstacle to the exportation, by the Ohío and the Mississippi, of provisions from the part of Virginia which it waters. Its banks are inhabited, but less than those of the Ohio.

CHAP. XI.

Gallipoli.—State of the French colony Scioto.—Alexandria at the mouth of the Great Scioto.—Arrival at Limestone in Kentucky.

GALLIPOLI is situated four miles below Point Pleasant, on the right bank of the Ohio. At this place assembled nearly a fourth part of the French, who, in 1789 and 1790, left their country to go and settle at Scioto: but it was not till after a sojourn of fifteen months at Alexandria in Virginia, where they waited the termination of the war with the savages, that they could take possession of the lands which they had bought so dearly. They were even on the point of being dispossessed of them, on account of the disputes that arose between the Scioto Company and that of the Ohio, of whom the former had primitively purchased these estates; but scarcely had they arrived upon the soil that was destined for them when the war broke out afresh between the Americans and Indians, and ended in the destruction of those unfortunate colonies. There is no doubt that, alone and destitute of support, they would have been all massacred, had it not been for the predilection which all the Indian nations round Canada and Louisiana have for the French. Again, as long as they did not take an active part in that war, they were not disturbed: but the American army having gained a signal advantage near the *embouchure* of the Great Kenaway, and crossed the Ohio, the inhabitants of Gallipoli were united to it. From that time they were no longer protected, nor could they stir out of the inclosure of their village. Out of two that had strayed not more than two hundred yards, one was scalped and murdered, and the other carried a prisoner a great distance into the interior. When I was at Gallipoli they had just heard from him. He gained his livelihood very comfortably by repairing guns, and exercising his trade as a goldsmith in the Indian village where he lived, and did not express the least wish to return with his countrymen.

The war being terminated, the congress, in order to indemnify these unfortunate Frenchmen for the successive losses which they had sustained, gave them twenty thousand acres of land situated between the small rivers Sandy and Scioto, seventy miles lower than Gallipoli. These twenty thousand acres were at the rate of two hundred and ten acres to every family. Those among them who had neither strength nor resolution enough to go a second time, without any other support than that of their children, to isolate themselves amidst the woods, hew down, burn, and root up the lower parts of trees, which are frequently more than five feet in diameter, and afterward split them to inclose their fields, sold their lots to the Americans or Frenchmen that were somewhat more enterprising. Thirty families only went to settle in their new possessions. Since the three or four years that they have resided there they have succeeded, by dint of labour, in forming for themselves tolerable establishments, where, by the help of a soil excessively fertile, they have an abundant supply of provisions; at least I conceived so, when I was there.

Gallipoli, situated on the borders of the Ohio, is composed solely of about sixty log-houses, most of which being uninhabited, are falling into ruins; the rest are occupied by Frenchmen, who breathe out a miserable existence. Two only among them appear to enjoy the smallest ray of comfort: the one keeps an inn, and distills brandy from peaches, which he sends to Kentucky, or sells it at a tolerable advantage: the other, M. Burau, from Paris, by whom I was well entertained, though unacquainted with him. Nothing can equal the perseverance of this Frenchman, whom the nature of his commerce obliges continually to travel over the banks of the Ohio, and to make, once or twice a year, a journey of four or five hundred miles through the woods, to go to the towns situated beyond the Alleghany Mountains. I learnt from him that the intermittent fevers, which at first had added to the calamities of the inhabitants of Gallipoli, had not shown itself for upwards of three years. That, however, did not prevent a dozen of them going lately to New Orleans in quest of a better fortune, but almost all of them died of the yellow fever the first year after their arrival.

Such was the situation of the establishment of Scioto when I was there. Though they did not succeed better, it is not that the French are less persevering and industrious than the Americans and Germans; it is that among those who departed for Scioto not a tenth part were fit for the toils they were destined to endure. However, it was not politic of the speculators, who sold land at five shillings an acre, which at that time was not worth one in America, to acquaint those whom they induced to purchase that they would be obliged, for the two first years, to have an axe in their hands nine hours a day; or that a good wood-cutter, having nothing but his hands, would be sooner at his ease on those fertile borders, but which he must, in the first place, clear, than he who, arriving there with two or three hundred guineas in his purse, is unaccustomed to such kind of labour. This cause, independent of the war with the natives, was more than sufficient to plunge the new colonists in misery, and stifle the colony in its birth.

On the 25th of July we set out from Gallipoli for Alexandria, which is about a hundred and four miles distant, and arrived there in three days and a half. The ground designed for this town is at the mouth of the Great Scioto, and in the angle which the right bank of this river forms with the north west border of the Ohio. Although the plan of Alexandria has been laid out these many years, nobody goes to settle there; and the number of its houses is not more than twenty, the major part of which are log-houses. Notwithstanding its situation is very favourable with regard to the numerous settlements already formed beyond the new town upon the Great Scioto, whose banks, not so high, and more marshy, are, it is said, nearly as fertile as those of the Ohio. The population would be much more considerable, if the inhabitants were not subject, every autumn, to intermittent fevers, which seldom abate till the approach of winter. This part of the country is the most unwholesome of all those that compose the immense state of Ohio. The seat of government belonging to this new state is at Chillicotha, which contains about a hundred and fifty houses, and is situated sixty miles from the mouth of the Great Scioto. A weekly newspaper is published there.

At Alexandria, and the other little towns in the western country, which are situated upon a very rich soil, the space between every house is almost entirely covered with *stramonium*. This dangerous and disagreeable plant has propagated surprisingly in every part where the earth has been uncovered and cultivated within twelve or fifteen years; and let the inhabitants do what they will, it spreads still wider every year. It is generally supposed to have made its appearance at James-Town in Virginia, whence it derived the name of *James-weed.* Travellers use it to heal the wounds made on horses' backs occasioned by the rubbing of the saddle.

Mullein is the second European plant that I found very abundant in the United States, although in a less proportion than the *stramonium.* It is very common on the road leading from Philadelphia to Lancaster, but less so past the town; and I saw no more of it beyond the Alleghany Mountains.

On the 1st of April we arrived at Limestone in Kentucky, fifty miles lower than Alexandria. There ended my travels on the Ohio. We had come three hundred and forty-eight miles in a canoe from Wheeling, and had taken ten days to perform the journey, during which we were incessantly obliged to paddle, on account of the slowness of the stream. This labour, although painful, at any rate, to those who are unaccustomed to it, was still more so on account of the intense heat. We also suffered much from thirst, not being able to procure any thing to drink but by stopping at the plantations on the banks of the river; for in summer the water of the Ohio acquires such a degree of heat, that it is not fit to be drank till it has been kept twenty-four hours. This excessive heat is occasioned, on the one hand, by the extreme heat of the climate in that season of the year, and on the other, by the slow movement of the stream.

I had fixed on the 1st of October to be the epoch of my return to Charleston in South Carolina, and I had nearly a thousand miles to go by land before I could arrive there, in executing the design I had formed of travelling through the state of Tennessea, which lengthened my route considerably. Pressed for time, I relinquished the intention I had formed of going farther down the Ohio, and took leave of Mr. Samuel Craft, who pursued by himself, in a canoe, his journey to Louisville, whence, after having come down the Ohio and Mississippi, he was to proceed up the river Yazous to go to Natches, and then return by land to the state of Vermont, where he expected to be about the middle of November following, after having made, in six months, a circuit of nearly four thousand miles.

CHAP. XII.

Fish and shells of the Ohio—Inhabitants on the Banks of the river—Agriculture—American Emigrant—Commercial Intelligence relative to that part of the United States.

THE banks of the Ohio, although elevated from twenty to sixty feet, scarcely afford any strong substances from Pittsburgh; and except large detached stones of a greyish colour and very soft, that we observed in an extent of ten or twelve miles below Wheeling, the remainder part seems vegetable earth. A few miles before we reached Limestone we began to observe a bank of a chalky nature, the thickness of which being very considerable, left no room to doubt but what it must be of a great extent.

Two kinds of flint, roundish and of a middling size, furnished the bed of the Ohio abundantly, especially as we approached the isles, where they are accumulated by the strength of the current; some of a darkish hue, break easily; others smaller, and in less quantities, are three parts white, and scarcely transparent.

In the Ohio, as well as in the Alleghany, Monangahela, and other rivers in the west, they find in abundance a species of *Mulette* which is from five to six inches in length. They do not eat it, but the mother-o'-pearl which is very thick in it, is used in making buttons. I have seen some at Lexinton which were as beautiful as those they make in Europe. This new species which I brought over with me, has been described by Mr. Bosc, under the name of the *Unio Ohiotensis.*

The Ohio abounds in fish of different kinds; the most common is the cat-fish, or *silurus felis,* which is generally caught with a line, and weighs sometimes a hundred pounds. The first fold of the upper fins of this fish are strong and pointed, similar to those of a perch, which he makes use of to kill others of a lesser size. He swims several inches under the one he wishes to attack, then rising rapidly, he pierces him several times in the belly; this we had an opportunity of observing twice in the course of our navigation. This fish is also taken with a kind of spear.

Till the years 1796 and 1797 the banks of the Ohio were so little populated that they scarcely consisted of thirty families in the space of four hundred miles; but since that epoch a great number of emigrants have come from the mountainous parts of Pennsylvania and Virginia, and settled there; in consequence of which the plantations now are so increased, that they are not farther than two or three miles distant from each other, and when on the river we always had a view of some of them.

The inhabitants on the borders of the Ohio, employ the greatest part of their time in stag and bear hunting, for the sake of the skins, which they dispose of. The taste that they have contracted for this kind of life is prejudicial to the culture of their lands; besides they have scarcely any time to meliorate their new possessions, that usually consist of two or three hundred acres, of which not more than eight or ten are cleared. Nevertheless, the produce that they derive from them, with the milk of their cows, is sufficient for themselves and families, which are always very numerous. The houses that they inhabit are built upon the borders of the river, generally in a pleasant situation, whence they enjoy the most delightful prospects; still their mode of building does not correspond with the beauties of the spot, being nothing but miserable log houses, without windows, and so small that two beds occupy the greatest part of them. Notwithstanding two men may erect and finish, in less than three days, one of these habitations, which, by their diminutive size and sorry appearance, seem rather to belong to a country where timber is very scarce, instead of a place that abounds with forests. The inhabitants on the borders of the Ohio do not hesitate to receive travellers who claim their hospitality; they give them a lodging, that is to say, they permit them to sleep upon the floor wrapped up in their rugs. They are accommodated with bread, Indian corn, dried ham, milk and butter, but seldom any thing else; at the same time the price of provisions is very moderate in this part of the United States, and all through the western country.

No attention is paid by the inhabitants to any thing else but the culture of Indian corn; and although it is brought to no great perfection, the soil being so full of roots, the stems are from ten to twelve feet high, and produce from twenty to thirty-five hundred weight of corn per acre. For the three first years after the ground is cleared, the corn springs up too strong, and scatters before it ears, so that they cannot sow in it for four or five years after, when the ground is cleared of the stumps and roots that were left in at first. The Americans in the interior cultivate corn rather through speculation to send the flour to the sea-ports, than for their own consumption; as nine tenths of them eat no other bread but that made from Indian corn; they make loaves of it from eight to ten pounds, which they bake in ovens, or small cakes baked on a board before the fire. This bread is generally eaten hot, and is not very palatable to those who are not used to it.

The peach is the only fruit tree that they have as yet cultivated, which thrives so rapidly that it produces fruit after the second year.

The price of the best land on the borders of the Ohio did not exceed three piastres per acre; at the same time it is not so dear on the left bank in the States of Virginia and Kentucky, where the settlements are not looked upon as quite so good.

The two banks of the Ohio, properly speaking, not having been inhabited above eight or nine years, nor the borders of the rivers that run into it, the Americans who are settled there, share but very feebly in the commerce that is carried on through the channel of the Mississippi. This commerce consists at present in hams and salted pork, brandies distilled from corn and peaches, butter, hemp, skins and various sorts of flour. They send again cattle to the Atlantic States. Trades-people who supply themselves at Pittsburgh and Wheeling, and go up and down the river in a canoe, convey them haberdashery goods, and more especially tea and coffee, taking some of their produce in return.

More than half of those who inhabit the borders of the Ohio, are again the first inhabitants, or as they are called in the United States, the *first settlers*, a kind of men who cannot settle upon the soil that they have cleared, and who under pretence of finding a better land, a more wholesome country, a greater abundance of game, push forward, incline perpetually towards the most distant points of the American population, and go and settle in the neighbourhood of the savage nations, whom they brave even in their own country. Their ungenerous mode of treating them stirs up frequent broils, that brings on bloody wars, in which they generally fall victims;

rather on account of their being so few in number, than through defect of courage.

Prior to our arrival at Marietta, we met one of these *settlers*, an inhabitant of the environs of Wheeling, who accompanied us down the Ohio, and with whom we travelled for two days. Alone in a canoe from eighteen to twenty feet long, and from twelve to fifteen inches broad, he was going to survey the borders of the Missouri* for a hundred and fifty miles beyond its *embouchure*. The excellent quality of the land that is reckoned to be more fertile there than that on the borders of the Ohio, and which the Spanish government at that time ordered to be distributed *gratis*, the quantity of beavers, elks, and more especially bisons, were the motives that induced him to emigrate into this remote part of the country, whence after having determined on a suitable spot to settle there with his family, he was returning to fetch them from the borders of the Ohio, which obliged him to take a journey of fourteen or fifteen hundred

* The banks of this river are now inhabited by the Americans, for forty miles beyond its *embouchure* in the Mississippi; the number of thoſe who are ſettled there is computed to be about three thouſand, and it increaſes daily by the repeated emigrations that are made from Kentucky and the Upper Carolinas.

miles, his costume, like that of all the American sportsmen, consisted of a waistcoat with sleeves, a pair of pantaloons, and a large red and yellow worsted sash. A carabine, a tomahawk or little axe, which the Indians make use of to cut wood and to terminate the existence of their enemies, two beaver-snares, and a large knife suspended at his side, constituted his sporting dress. A rug comprised the whole of his luggage. Every evening he encamped on the banks of the river, where, after having made a fire, he passed the night; and whenever he conceived the place favourable for the chace, he remained in the woods for several days together, and with the produce of his sport, he gained the means of subsistence, and new ammunition with the skins of the animals that he had killed.

Such were the first inhabitants of Kentucky and Tennessea, of whom there are now remaining but very few. It was they who began to clear those fertile countries, and wrested them from the savages who ferociously disputed their right; it was they, in short, who made themselves masters of the possessions, after five or six years' bloody war: but the long habit of a wandering and idle life has prevented their enjoying the fruit of their labours, and profiting by the very price to which these lands have risen in so short a time. They have emigrated to more remote parts of the country, and formed new settlements. It will be the same with most of those who inhabit the borders of the Ohio. The same inclination that led them there will induce them to emigrate from it. To the latter will succeed fresh emigrants, coming also from the Atlantic states, who will desert their possessions to go in quest of a milder climate and a more fertile soil. The money that they will get for them will suffice to pay for their new acquisitions, the peaceful delight of which is assured by a numerous population. The last comers instead of loghouses, with which the present inhabitants are contented, will build wooden ones, clear a greater quantity of the land, and be as industrious and persevering in the melioration of their new possessions as the former were indolent in every thing, being so fond of hunting. To the culture of Indian corn they will add that of other grain, hemp, and tobacco; rich pasturages will nourish innumerable flocks, and an advantageous sale of all the country's produce will be assured them through the channel of the Ohio.

The happy situation of this river entitles it to be looked upon as the centre of commercial activity between the eastern and western states. By it the latter receive the manufactured goods which Europe, India, and the Caribbees supply the former; and it is the only open communication with the ocean, for the exportation of provisions from the immense and fertile part of the United States comprised between the Alleghany Mountains, the lakes, and the left banks of the Mississippi.

All these advantages, blended with the salubrity of the climate and the beauty of the landscapes, enlivened in the spring by a group of boats which the current whirls along with an astonishing rapidity, and the uncommon number of sailing vessels that from the bosom of this vast continent go directly to the Caribbees; all these advantages, I say, make me think that the banks of the Ohio, from Pittsburgh to Louisville inclusively, will, in the course of twenty years, be the most populous and commercial part of the United States, and where I should settle in preference to any other.

CHAP. XIII.

Limestone.—Route from Limestone to Lexinton.—Washington.—Salt-works at Mays-Lick.—Millesburgh.—Paris.

LIMESTONE, situated upon the left bank of the Ohio, consists only of about thirty or forty houses, constructed with wood. This little town, built upwards of fifteen years, one would imagine to be more extensive. It has long been the place where all the emigrants landed who came from the Northern States by the way of Pittsburgh, and is still the staple for all sorts of merchandize sent from Philadelphia and Baltimore to Kentucky.

The travellers who arrive at Limestone by the Ohio find great difficulty in procuring horses on hire, to go to the places of their destination. The inhabitants there, as well as at Shippensburgh, take this undue advantage, in order to sell them at an enormous price. As I intended staying some time at Lexinton, which would greatly enhance my expenses, I resolved to travel there on foot; upon which I left my portmanteau with the landlord of the inn where I stopped, which he undertook for a piaster to send me to Lexinton, and I set off the same day. It is reckoned from Limestone to Lexinton to be sixty-five miles, which I went in two days and a half. The first town we came to was Washington, which was only four miles off. It is much larger than Limestone, and contains about two hundred houses, all of wood, and built on both sides of the road. Trade is very brisk there; it consists principally in corn, which is exported to New Orleans. There are several very fine plantations in the environs, the land of which is as well cultivated and the enclosures as well constructed, as at Virginia and Pennsylvania. I went seven miles the first evening, and on the following day reached Springfield, composed of five or six houses, among the number of which are two spacious inns, well built, where the inhabitants of the environs assemble together. Thence I passed through Mays-Lick, where there is a salt-mine. I stopped there to examine the process pursued for the extraction of salt. The wells that supply the salt water are about twenty feet in depth, and not more than fifty or sixty fathoms from the river Salt-Lick, the waters of which are somewhat brackish in summer time. For evaporation they make use of brazen pots, containing about two hundred pints, and similar in form to those used in France for making lye. They put ten or a dozen of them in a row on a pit four feet in depth, and a breadth proportionate to their diameter, so that the sides lay upon the edge of the pit, supported by a few handfuls of white clay, which fill up but very imperfectly the spaces between the vessels. The wood, which they cut in billets of about three feet, is thrown in at the extremities of the pit. These sort of kilns are extravagant, and consume a prodigious quantity of wood; I made an observation of it to the people employed in the business, to which they made answer, that they did not know there was any preferable mode; and they should follow their own till some person or other from the Old Country (meaning Europe) came and taught them to do better. The scarcity of hands for the cutting down and conveyance of the wood, and the few saline principles that the water contains when dissolved, occasions the salt to be very dear; they sell it at from four to five piasters per hundred weight. It is that scarcity which induces many of them to search for salt springs. They are usually found in places described by the name of Licks, where the bisons, elks, and stags that existed in Kentucky before the arrival of the Europeans, went by hundreds to lick the saline particles with which the soil is impregnated. There are in this state and that of Tenessea a set of quacks, who by means of a hazle wand pretend to discover springs of salt and fresh water; but they are only consulted by the more ignorant class of people, who never send for them but when they are induced by some circumstance or other to search over a spot of ground where they suspect one of those springs.

The country we traversed ten miles on this side Mays-Lick, and eight miles beyond, did not afford the least vestige of a plantation. The soil is dry and sandy; the road is covered with immense flat chalky stones, of a bluish cast inside, the edges of which are round. The only trees that we observed were the white oak, or *quercus alba*, and nut-tree, or *juglans hickery*, but their stinted growth and wretched appearance clearly indicated the sterility of the soil, occasioned, doubtless, by the salt mines that it contains.

From Mays-Lick I went to Millesburgh, composed of fifty houses; I went there to visit Mr. Savary, who had been very intimately acquainted with my father, and by his invitation I left my inn and went to lodge at his house. Mr. Savary is one of the greatest proprietors in that part of the country; he possesses more than eighty thousand acres of land in Virginia, Tenessea and Kentucky. The taxes that he pays, although moderate, are notwithstanding very burthensome to him; more so, as it is with the greatest difficulty he can find purchasers for his land, as the emigrations of the eastern states, having taken a different direction, incline but very feebly towards Kentucky.

Near Millesburgh flows a little river, from five to six fathoms broad, upon which two saw-mills are erected. The stream was then so low that I crossed it upon large chalky stones, which comprised a part of its bottom, and which at that time were above water. In winter time, on the contrary, it swells to such a degree that it can scarcely be passed by means of a bridge twenty-five feet in height. The bridges thrown over the small rivers, or creeks, that are met with frequently in the interior of the country, more especially in the eastern states, are all formed of the trunks of trees placed transversely by each other. These bridges have no railings; and whenever a person travels on horseback, it is always prudent to alight in order to cross them.

On this side Lexinton we passed through Paris, a manor-house for the county of Bourbon. This small town, in the year 1796, consisted of no more than eighteen houses, and now contains more than a hundred and fifty, half of which are brick. It is situated on a delightful plain, and watered by a small river, near which are several corn mills. Every thing seems to announce the comfort of its inhabitants. Seven or eight were drinking whiskey at a respectable inn where I stopped to refresh myself on account of the excessive heat. After having replied to different questions which they asked me concerning the intent of my journey, one of them invited me to dine with him, wishing to introduce me to one of my fellow-countrymen arrived lately from Bengal. I yielded to his entreaties, and actually found a Frenchman who had left Calcutta to go and reside at Kentucky. He was settled at Paris, where he exercised the profession of a school-master.

CHAP. XIV.

Lexinton.—Manufactories established there.—Commerce.—Dr. Samuel Brown.

LEXINTON, the manor-house for the county of Fayette, is situated in the midst of a flat soil of about three hundred acres, like the rest of the small towns of the United States that are not upon the borders of the sea. This town is traced upon a regular plan, and its streets, sufficiently broad, cut each other at right angles. The want of pavement renders it very muddy in winter time, and rainy weather. The houses, most of which are brick, are disseminated upon an extent of eighty or a hundred acres, except those which form the main street, where they are contiguous to each other. This town, founded in 1780, is the oldest and most wealthy of the three new western states; it contains about three thousand inhabitants. Frankfort, the seat of government in Kentucky, which is upwards of twenty miles distant from it, is not so populous. We may attribute the rapid increase of Lexinton to its situation in the centre of one of the most fertile parts of the country, comprised in a kind of semi-circle, formed by the Kentucky river.

There are two printing-offices at Lexinton, in each of which a newspaper is published twice a week. Part of the paper is manufactured in the country, and is dearer by one-third than in France. That which they use for writing. originally imported from England, comes by the way of Philadelphia and Baltimore. Two extensive rope walks, constantly in employ, supply the ships with rigging that are built upon the Ohio. On the borders of the little river that runs very near the town several tan-yards are established that supply the wants of the inhabitants. I observed at the gates of these tan-yards strong leathers of a yellowish cast, tanned with the black oak; in consequence of which I saw that this tree grew in Kentucky, although I had not observed it between Limestone and Lexinton; in fact, I had seen nothing but land either parched up or extremely fertile; and, as I have since observed, this tree grows in neither, it is an inhabitant of the mountainous parts, where the soil is gravelly and rather moist.

The want of hands excites the industry of the inhabitants of this country. When I was at Lexinton one of them had just obtained a patent for a nail machine, more complete and expeditious than the one made use of in the prisons at New York and Philadelphia; and a second announced one for the grinding and cleaning of hemp and sawing wood and stones. This machine, moved by a horse or a current of water, is capable, according to what the inventor said, to break and clean eight thousand weight of hemp per day.

The articles manufactured at Lexinton are very passable, and the speculators are ever said to make rapid fortunes, notwithstanding the extreme scarcity of hands. This scarcity proceeds from the inhabitants giving so decided a preference to agriculture, that there are very few of them who put their children to any trade, wanting their services in the field. The following comparison will more clearly prove this scarcity of artificers in the western states: At Charleston in Carolina, and at Savannah in Georgia, a cabinet-maker, carpenter, mason, tinman, tailor, shoemaker, &c. earns two piastres a day, and cannot live for less than six per week; at New York and Philadelphia he has but one piaster, and it costs him four per week. At Marietta, Lexinton and Nasheville, in Tenessea, these workmen earn from one piaster to one and a half a day, and can subsist a week with the produce of one day's labour. Another example may tend to give an idea of the low price of provisions in the western states. The boarding-house, where I lived during my stay at Lexinton, passes for one of the best in the town, and we were profusely served at the rate of two piastres per week. I am informed that living is equally cheap in the states of New England, which comprise Connecticut, Massachusets, and New Hampshire; but the price of labour is not so high, and therefore more proportionate to the price of provisions.

Independent of those manufactories which are established in Lexinton, there are several common potteries, and one or two powder-mills, the produce of which is consumed in the country or exported to Upper Carolina and Low Louisiana. The sulphur is obtained from Philadelphia and the saltpetre is manufactured in the country; the materials are extracted from the grottos, or caverns, that are found on the declivity of lofty hills in the most mountainous part of the state. The soil there is extremely rich in nitrous particles, which is evidently due to the chalky rock, at the expense of which all these excavations are formed, as well as for vegetable substances, which are casually thrust into their interior. This appears to demonstrate that the assimilation of animal matters is not absolutely necessary, even in the formation of artificial nitrous veins, to produce a higher degree of nitrification. Saltpetre of the first preparation is sold at about sixpence halfpenny per pound. Among the various samples I have seen, I never observed the least appearance of marine salt. The process that is used is as defective as their preparation of salt; I only speak relative to the extraction of the saltpetre, not having seen the powder-mills. I shall conclude by observing, that it is only in Kentucky and Tenessea that saltpetre is manufactured, and not in the Atlantic States.

The majority of the inhabitants of Lexinton trade with Kentucky; they receive their merchandize from Philadelphia and Baltimore in thirty-five or forty days, including the journey of two days and a half from Limestone, where they land all the goods destined for Kentucky. The price of carriage is from seven to eight piastres per hundred weight. Seven-tenths of the manufactured articles consumed in Kentucky, as well as in the other parts of the

United States, are imported from England; they consist chiefly in coarse and fine jewellery, cutlery, ironmongery, and tin ware; in short, drapery, mercery, drugs, and fine earthenware, muslins, nankeens, tea, &c. are imported directly from India to the United States by the American vessels; and they get from the Carribbees coffee, and various kinds of raw sugar, as none but the poorer class of the inhabitants make use of maple sugar.

The French goods that are sent into this part of the country are reduced to a few articles in the silk line, such as taffetas, silk stockings, &c. also brandies and mill-stones, notwithstanding their enormous weight, and the distance from the sea ports.

From Lexinton the different kinds of merchandize are despatched into the interior of the state, and the overplus is sent by land into Tenessea. It is an easy thing for merchants to make their fortunes; in the first place, they usually have a twelvemonth's credit from the houses at Philadelphia and Baltimore, and in the next, as there are so few, they are always able to fix in their favour the course of colonial produce, which they take in exchange for their goods: as, through the extreme scarcity of specie, most of these transactions are done by way of barter; the merchants, however, use every exertion in their power to get into their possession the little specie in circulation; it is only particular articles that are sold for money, or in exchange for produce the sale of which is always certain, such as the linen of the country, or hemp. Payments in money always bear a difference of fifteen or twenty per cent to the merchant's profits. All the specie collected in the course of trade is sent by land to Philadelphia; I have seen convoys of this kind that consisted of fifteen or twenty horses *. The trouble of conveyance is so great that they give the preference to Bank bills of the United States, which bear a discount of two per cent. The merchants in all parts take them, but the inhabitants of the country will not, through fear of their being forged. I must again remark, that there is not a single species of colonial produce in Kentucky, except *gensing*, that will bear the expense of carriage by land from that state to Philadelphia; as it is demonstrated that twenty-five pounds weight

* The distance from Lexinton to Philadelphia, by way of Pennsylvania, is about six hundred and fifty miles. Those who have occasion to go there on business, generally set out in autumn, and take three weeks or a month to perform the journey.

would cost more expediting that way, even going up the Ohio, than a thousand by that river, without reckoning the passage by sea, although we have had repeated examples that the passage from New Orleans to Philadelphia or New York is sometimes as long as that from France to the United States.

The current coin in the states of Kentucky and Tennessea has the same divisions as in Virginia They reckon six shillings to the dollar or piastre. The hundreds, which nearly correspond with our halfpence, although having a forced currency, do not appear in circulation. The quarters, eighths, and sixteenths of a piastre form the small white money. As it is extremely scarce, it is supplied by a very indifferent method, but which appears necessary, and consists in cutting the dollars into pieces. As every body is entitled to make this division, there are people who do it for the sake of gain; at the same time in the retail trade the seller will generally abate in his articles for a whole dollar, than have their full worth in six or eight pieces.

I have heard from several persons very well informed, that during the last war, corn being kept up at an exorbitant rate, it was computed that the exportations from Kentucky had balanced the price of the importations of English goods from Philadelphia and Baltimore, by the way of the Ohio: but since the peace, the demand for flour and salt provisions having ceased in the Caribbees, corn has fallen considerably; so that the balance of trade is wholly unfavourable to the country.

During my stay at Lexinton I frequently saw Dr. Samuel Brown, from Virginia, a physician of the college of Edinburgh, and member of the Philosophical Society, to whom several members of that society had given me letters of recommendation. A merited reputation undeniably places Dr. S. Brown in the first rank of physicians settled in that part of the country. Receiving regularly the scientific journals from London, he is always in the channel of new discoveries, and turns them to the advantage of his fellow-citizens. It is to him that they are indebted for the introduction of the cow-pox. He had at that time inoculated upward of five hundred persons in Kentucky, when they were making their first attempts in New York and Philadelphia. Dr. Brown also employs himself in collecting fossils and other natural productions, which abound in this interesting country. I have seen at his house several relics of very large unknown fish, caught in the

Kentucky River, and which were remarkable for their singular forms. The analysis of the mineral waters at Mud-Lick was to employ the first leisure time he had. These waters are about sixty miles from Lexinton; they are held in great esteem, and the most distinguished personages in the country were drinking them when I was in the town. The Philosophical Transactions and the Monthly Review, published at New York by Dr. Mitchel, are the periodical works wherein Dr. Brown inserts the fruit of his observation and research.

I had also the pleasure of forming an acquaintance with several French gentlemen settled in that part of the country: Mr. Robert, to whom I was recommended by Mr. Marbois, jun. then in the United States; and Messrs. Duhamel and Mentelle, sons of the members of the National Institution of the same name. The two latter are settled in the environs of Lexinton; the first as a physician, and the second as a farmer. I received from them that marked attention and respect so pleasing to a foreigner at a distance from his country and his friends; in consequence of which I now feel myself happy in having this means of publicly expressing my warmest gratitude.

CHAP. XV.

Departure from Lexinton.—Culture of the vine at Kentucky.—Passage over the Kentucky and Dick Rivers.—Departure for Nasheville.—Mulder Hill. —Passage over Green River.

I SET out on the 10th of August from Lexinton to Nasheville, in the state of Tennessea; and as the establishment formed to naturalize the vine in Kentucky was but a few miles out of my road, I resolved to go and see it. There is no American but what takes the warmest interest in attempts of that kind, and several persons in the Atlantic states had spoken to me of the success which had crowned this undertaking. French vines being one of the principal articles of our commerce with the United States, I wished to be satisfied respecting the degree of prosperity which this establishment might have acquired.

In the mean time, from the indifferent manner which I had heard it spoken of in the country I suspected beforehand that the first attempts had not been very fortunate.

About fourteen miles from Lexinton I quitted the Hickman Ferry road, turned on my left, and strolled into the woods, so that I did not reach the vineyard till the evening, when I was handsomely received by Mr. Dufour, who superintends the business. He gave me an invitation to sleep, and spend the following day with him, which I accepted.

There reigns in the United States a public spirit that makes them greedily seize hold of every plan that tends to enrich the country by agriculture and commerce. That of rearing the vine in Kentucky was eagerly embraced. Several individuals united together, and formed a society to put it in execution, and it was decreed that a fund should be established of ten thousand dollars, divided into two hundred shares of fifty dollars each. This fund was very soon accomplished. Mr. Dufour, the chief of a small Swiss colony which seven or eight years before had settled in Kentucky, and who had proposed this undertaking, was deputed to search for a proper soil, to procure vine plants, and to do every thing he might think necessary to insure success. The spot that he has chosen and cleared is on the Kentucky river, about twenty miles from Lexinton. The soil is excellent, and the vineyard is planted upon the declivity of a hill exposed to the south, and the base of which is about two hundred fathoms from the river.

Mr. Dufour intended to go to France to procure the vine plants, and with that idea went to New York; but the war, or other causes that I know not, prevented his setting out, and he contented himself with collecting, in this town and Philadelphia, slips of every species that he could find in the possession of individuals that had them in their gardens. After unremitted labour he made a collection of twenty-five different sorts, which he brought to Kentucky, where he employed himself in cultivating them. However the success did not answer the expectation; only four or five various kinds survived, among which were those that he had described by the name of Burgundy and Madeira, but the former is far from being healthy. The grape generally decays before it is ripe. When I saw them the bunches were thin and poor, the berries small, and every thing announced that the vintage of 1802 would not be more abundant than that of the preceding years. The Madeira vines appeared, on the contrary, to give some hopes. Out of a hundred and fifty or two hundred, there was a third loaded with very fine bunches. The whole of these vines do not occupy a space of more than six acres. They are planted and fixed with props similar to those in the environs of Paris.

Such was then the situation of this establishment, in which the stockholders concerned themselves but very little. It was again about to experience another check by the division of Mr. Dufour's family, one part of which was on the point of setting out to the banks of the Ohio, there to form a settlement. These particulars are sufficient to give, on the pretended flourishing state of the vines in Kentucky, an idea very different to that which might be formed from the pompous account of them which appeared some months since in our public papers.

I profited by my stay with Mr. Dufour, to ask him in what part of Kentucky the numerous emigration of his countrymen had settled, which had been so much spoken of in our newspapers in 1793 and 1794? His reply was, that a great number of the Swiss had actually formed an intention to settle there; but just as they were setting out, the major part had changed their mind, and that the colony was then reduced to his family and a few friends, forming, in the whole, eleven persons.

I did not set out from the vineyard till the second day after my arrival. Mr. Dufour offered, in order to shorten my journey, to conduct me through the wood where they cross the Kentucky river. I accepted his proposal, and although the distance was only four miles we took two hours to accomplish it, as we were obliged to alight either to climb up or descend the mountains, or to leap our horses over the trunks of old trees piled one upon another. The soil, as fertile as in the environs of Lexinton, will be difficult to cultivate, on account of the great inequality of the ground. Beech, nut, and oak trees, form chiefly the mass of the forests. We crossed, in the mean time, the shallows of the river, covered exclusively with beautiful palms. A great number of people in the country dread the proximity of these palms; they conceive that the down which grows on the reverse of the leaves, in spring, and which falls off in the course of the summer, brings on consumptions, by producing an irritation of the lungs, almost insensible, but continued.

In this season of the year the Kentucky River is so low at Hickman Ferry that a person may ford it with the greatest ease.

I stopped a few minutes at the inn where the ferry-boat plies when the water is high, and while they were giving my horse some corn I went on the banks of the river to survey it more attentively. Its borders are formed by an enormous mass of chalky stones, remarkably peaked, about a hundred and fifty feet high, and which bear, from the bottom to the top, evident traces of the action of the waters, which have washed them away in several parts. A broad and long street, where the houses are arranged in a right line, will give an idea of the channel of this river at Hickman Ferry. It swells amazingly in spring and autumn, and its waters rise at that time, in a few days, from sixty to seventy feet.

I met, at this inn, an inhabitant of the country who lived about sixty miles farther up. This gentleman, with whom I entered into conversation, and who appeared to me to enjoy a comfortable existence, gave me strong invitations to pass a week with him at his house; and as he supposed that I was in quest of a spot to form a settlement, which is usually the intention of those who go to Kentucky, he offered his services to shew me a healthy soil, wishing very much, he said, to have an inhabitant of the old country for a neighbour. It has often happened to me, in this state as well as in that of Tennessea, to refuse similar propositions by strangers whom I met at the inns or at the houses where I asked a lodging, and who invited me, after that, to spend a few days in their family.

About a mile from Kentucky I left the Danville road, and took that of Harrod's Burgh, to go to General Adair, to whom Dr. Ramsey of Charleston had given me a letter of recommendation. I arrived at his house the same day. I crossed Dick's River, which is not half so broad as the Kentucky, but is extremely pleasant at this season of the year. Its bed is uniformly hollowed out by nature, and seems cased with stone. Part of the right bank, opposite to the place where they land, discovers a beautiful rock of a chalky substance, more than two hundred and fifty feet in height. The stratum forms one continued mass, which does not present the smallest interval, and which is only distinguished by zones and parallels of a bluish cast, the colour of which contrasts with the whiteness of the towering pile. On leaving its summit, numerous furrows, hollowed in the rock, very near together, and which seem to run *ad infinitum*, are seen at different heights. These furrows have visibly been formed by the current of the river, which at distant epochs had its bed at these various levels. Dick's River, like the Kentucky, experiences, in the spring, an extraordinary increase of water. The stratum of vegetable earth which covers the rock does not appear to be more than two or three feet thick. Virginia cedars are very common there. This tree, which is fond of lofty places where the chalky substance is very near to the superficies of the soil, thrives very well; but other trees, such as the black oak, the hickery, &c. are stinted, and assume a miserable appearance.

General Adair was absent when I arrived at his plantation. His lady received me in the most obliging manner, and for five or six days that I staid with her I received every mark of attention and hospitality, as though I had been intimately acquainted with the family.

A spacious and commodious house, a number of black servants, equipages, every thing announced the opulence of the General, which it is well known is not always, in America, the appendage of those honoured with that title. His plantation is situated near Harrodsburgh in the county of Mercer. Magnificent peach orchards, immense fields of Indian wheat, surround the house. The soil there is extremely fertile, which shews itself by the largeness of the blades of corn, their extraordinary height, and the abundance of the crops, that yield annually thirty or forty hundred weight of corn per acre. The mass of the surrounding forests is composed of those species of trees that are found in the better sort of land, such as the *gleditia acanthus*, *guilandina dioica*, *ulmus viscosa*, *morus rubra*, *corylus*, *annona triloba*. In short, for several miles round the surface of the ground is flat, which is very rare in that country.

As I could not defer my travels any longer, I did not accept of Mrs. Adair's invitation, who entreated me to stay till her husband's return; and on the 20th of August I set out in order to continue my route toward Nasheville, very much regretting not having had it in my power to form an acquaintance with the General.

My first day's journey was upward of twenty miles, and in the evening I put up at the house of one Hays, who keeps a kind of inn about fifty miles from Lexinton. Harrodsburgh, which I passed through that day, at present consists only of about twenty houses, irregularly scattered, and built of wood. Twelve miles farther I regained, at Chaplain Fork, the road to Danville. In this space, which is uninhabited, the soil is excellent; but very unequal.

The second day I went nearly thirty miles, and stopped at an inn kept by a person of the name of Skeggs. Ten miles on this side is Mulder-Hill, a steep and lofty mountain that forms a kind of amphitheatre. From its summit the neighbouring country presents the aspect of an immense valley, covered with forests of an imperceptible extent, whence, as far as the eye can reach, nothing but a gloomy verdant space is seen, formed by the tops of the close-connected trees, and through which not the vestige of a plantation can be discerned. The profound silence that reigns in these woods, uninhabited by wild beasts, and the security of the place, forms an *ensemble* rarely to be met with in other countries. At the summit of Mulder-Hill the road divides, to unite again a few miles farther on. I took the left, and the first plantation that I reached was that of Mr. Macmahon, formerly professor of a college in Virginia, who came very lately to reside in this part of the country, where he officiates as a clergyman.

Skeggs's inn, where I stopped after having left Mulder-Hill, was the worst station that I took from Limestone to Nasheville. It was destitute of every kind of provision, and I was obliged to sleep on the floor, wrapped up in my rug, without having been able to procure a supper. As there was no stable in this plantation, I turned my horse into a peach-orchard for pasture. The fences that inclosed it were broken down, and fearing he would escape in the night, I put a bell on his neck, such as travellers carry with them when compelled to sleep in the woods. The peaches at that time were in full perfection, and I perceived that my horse had been feeding on them, from the immense quantity of kernels lying under three or four trees. This was very easy for him, as the branches, loaded with fruit, hung nearly to the ground.

About eight miles hence I forded Green River, which flows into the Ohio, after innumerable windings, and runs through a narrow valley not more than a mile in breadth. At the place where I crossed it it had not three of water in an extent from fifteen to twenty fathoms broad; but in the spring, the only epoch when it is navigable, the water rises about eighteen feet, as may be judged by the roots of the trees that adorn its banks, and which are stripped naked by the current. Beyond the river we regain the road, which for the space of two miles serpentines in that part of the valley which is on the left bank. The soil of these shallows is marshy and very fruitful, where the beech tree, among others, flourishes in great perfection. Its diameter is usually in proportion to its height, and its massy trunk sometimes rises twenty-five or thirty feet from the earth divested of a single branch. The soil occupied by these trees is considered by the inhabitants as the most difficult to clear.

CHAP. XVI.

Passage over the Barrens, or Meadows.—Plantations upon the Road.—The View they present.—Plants discovered there.—Arrival at Nasheville.

ABOUT ten miles from Green River flows the Little Barren, a small river, from thirty to forty feet in breadth; the ground in the environs is dry and barren, and produces nothing but a few Virginia cedars, two-leaved pines, and black oaks. A little beyond this commence the Barrens, or Kentucky Meadows. I went the first day thirteen miles across these meadows, and put up at the house of Mr. Williamson, near Bears-Wallow.

In the morning, before I left the place, I wanted to give my horse some water, upon which my host directed me to a spring about a quarter of a mile from the house, where his family was supplied; I wandered about for the space of two hours in search of this, when I discovered a plantation in a low and narrow valley, where I learnt that I had mistaken the path, and was obliged to return to the place from whence I came. The mistress of the house told me that she had resided in the Barrens upwards of three years, and that for eighteeen months prior to my going there she had not seen an individual; that, weary of living thus isolated, her husband had been more than two months from home in quest of another spot, towards the mouth of the Ohio. Such was the pretence for this removal, which made the third since the family left Virginia. A daughter about fourteen years of age, and two children considerably younger, were all the company she had; her house, on the other hand, was stocked abundantly with vegetables and corn.

This part of the Barrens that chance occasioned me to stroll over, was precisely similar to that I had traversed the day before. I found a spring in a cavity of an orbicular form, where it took me upwards of an hour to get half a pail of water for my horse. The time that I had thus employed, that which I had lost in wandering about, added to the intense heat, obliged me to shorten my route: in consequence of which I put up at Dripping Spring, about ten miles from Bears-Wallow.

On the following day, the 20th, I went twenty-eight miles, and stopped at the house of Mr. Jacob Kesly, belonging to the Dunker sect, which I discovered by his long beard. About ten miles from Dripping Spring I forded Big-Barren River, which appeared to me one third broader than Green River, the plantation of one Macfiddit, who plies a ferry-boat when the waters are high; and another, belonging to one Chapman. About three miles farther are the two oldest settlements on the road, both of them having been built upwards of fourteen years. When I was at this place, a boat laden with salt arrived from St. Genevieve, a French village situated upon the right bank of the Mississippi, about a hundred miles beyond the mouth of the Ohio.

My landlord's house was as miserably furnished as those I had lodged at for several days preceding, and I was again obliged to sleep on the floor. The major part of the inhabitants of Kentucky have been there too short a time to make any great improvements; they have a very indifferent supply of any thing except Indian corn and forage.

On the 27th of August I set off very early in the morning; and about thirteen miles from Mr. Kesley's I crossed the line that separates the State of Tennessea from that of Kentucky. There also terminates the Barrens; and to my great satisfaction I got into the woods. Nothing can be more tiresome than the doleful uniformity of these immense meadows where there is nobody to be met with; and where, except a great number of partridges, we neither see nor hear any species of living beings, and are still more isolated than in the middle of the forests.

The first plantation that I reached on entering Tennessea belonged to a person of the name of Checks, of whom I entertained a very indifferent opinion, by the conversation that he was holding with seven or eight of his neighbours, with whom he was drinking whiskey. Fearing lest I should witness some murdering scene or other, which among the inhabitants of this part of the country is frequently the end of intoxication, produced by this kind of spirits, I quickly took my leave, and put up at an inn about three miles farther off, where I found every accommodation. The late Duke of Orleans' son lodged at this house a few years before. On the day following I arrived at Nasheville, after having travelled twenty-seven miles.

The Barrens, or Kentucky Meadows, comprise an extent from sixty to seventy miles in length, by sixty miles in breadth. According to the signification of this word, I conceived I should have had to cross over a naked space, sown here and there with a few plants. I was confirmed in my opinion by that which some of the country people had given me of these meadows before I reached them. They told me that in this season I should perish with heat and thirst, and that I should not find the least shade the whole of the way, as the major part of the Americans who live in the woods have not the least idea that there is any part of the country entirely open, and still less that they could inhabit it. Instead of finding a country as it had been depicted to me, I was agreeably surprised to see a beautiful meadow, where the grass was from two to three feet high. Amidst these pasture lands I discovered a great variety of plants, among which were the *gerardia flava*, or gall of the earth; the *gnaphalium dioicum*, or white plantain; and the *rudbekia purpurea*. I observed that the roots of the latter plant participated in some degree with the sharp taste of the leaves of the *spi-*

lanthus oleracca. When I crossed these meadows the flower season was over with three parts of the plants, but the time for most of the seeds to ripen was still at a great distance; nevertheless I gathered about ninety different species of them which I took with me to France.

In some parts of the meadows we observed several species of the wild vine, and in particular that called by the inhabitants *summer grapes*, the bunches are as large, and the grapes of as good a quality as those in the vineyards round Paris, with this difference, that the berries are not quite so close together.

It seems to me that the attempts which have been made in Kentucky to establish the culture of the vine would have been more successful in the Barrens, the soil of which appears to me more adapted for this kind of culture than that on the banks of the Kentucky; the latter is richer it is true, at the same time the nature of the country, and the proximity of the forests render it much damper. This was also my father's opinion; he thought that the different parts of North America that he had travelled through, during a sojourn of twelve years, the States of Kentucky and Tennessea, and particularly the Barrens, were the parts in which the vine might be cultivated with the greatest success. His opinion was founded in a great measure upon the certainty that the vegetable stratum in the above states lies upon a chalky mass.

The Barrens are circumscribed by a wood about three miles broad, which in some parts joins to surrounding forests. The trees are in general very straggling, and at a greater distance from each other as they approach the meadows. On the side of Tennessea this border is exclusively composed of post oaks, or *quercus oblusiloba*, the wood of which being very hard, and not liable to rot, is, in preference to any other, used for fences. This serviceable tree would be easy to naturalize in France, as it grows among the pines in the worst of soil. We observed again, here and there, in the meadow, several black oaks, or *quercus nigra*; and nut trees, or *juglans kickery*, which rise about twelve or fifteen feet. Sometimes they formed small arbours, but always far enough apart from each other so as not to intercept the surrounding view. With the exception of small willows, about two feet high, *selix longirostris*, and a few *shumacs*, there is not the least appearance of a shrub. The surface of these meadows is generally very even; towards Dripping Spring I observed a lofty eminence, slightly adorned with trees, and bestrewed with enormous rocks, which hang jutting over the main road.

It appears there are a great number of subterraneous caverns in the Barrens, some of which are very near the surface. A short time before I was there, several pieces of the rocks that were decayed, fell with a tremendous crash into the road near Bears-Wallow, as a traveller was passing, who, by the greatest miracle escaped. We may easily conceive with what consequences such accidents must be attended in a country where the plantations are so distant from each other, and where, perhaps, a traveller does not pass for several days.

We remarked in these meadows several holes, widened at the top in the shape of funnels, the breadth of which varies according to their depth. In some of these holes, about five or six feet from the bottom, flows a small vein of water, which, in the same proportion as it fills, loses itself through another part. These kind of springs never fail; in consequence of which several of the inhabitants have been induced to settle in their vicinity; for, except the river Big-Barren, I did not see the smallest rivulet or creek; nor did I hear that they have ever attempted to dig wells; but were they to make the essay, I have no doubt of their success. According to the observations we have just made, the want of water, and wood adapted to make fences, will be long an obstacle to the increase of settlements in this part of Kentucky. Notwithstanding, one of these two inconveniences might be obviated, by changing the present mode of enclosing land, and substituting hedges, upon which the *gleditsia triacanthos*, one of the most common trees in the country, might be used with success. The Barrens at present are very thinly populated, considering their extent; for on the road where the plantations are closest together we counted but eighteen in a space of sixty or seventy miles.

Some of the inhabitants divide land of the Barrens in Kentucky into three classes, according to its quality. That which I crossed, where the soil is yellowish and rather gravelly, appeared to me the best adapted for the culture of corn. That of Indian wheat is almost the only thing to which the inhabitants apply themselves; but as the settlements are of a fresh date, the land has not been able to acquire that degree of prosperity that is observed on this side Mulder Hill. Most of the inhabitants who go to settle in the country, incline upon the skirts, or along the Little and Big Barren rivers, where they are attracted by the advantage that the meadows offer as pasture for the cattle, an advantage which, in a great measure, the inhabitants of the most fertile districts are deprived of, the country being so very woody, that there is scarcely any grass land to be seen.

Every year, in the course of the months of March or April, the inhabitants set fire to the grass, which at that time is dried up, and through its extreme length, would conceal from the cattle a fortnight or three weeks longer the new grass, which then begins to spring up. This custom is nevertheless generally censured; as being set on fire too early, the new grass is stripped of the covering that ought to shelter it from the spring and frosts, and in consequence of which its vegetation is retarded. The custom of burning the meadows was formerly practised by the natives, who came in this part of the country to hunt; in fact, they do it now in the other parts of North America, where there are *savannas* of an immense extent. Their aim in setting fire to it is to allure the stags, bisons, &c. into the parts which are burnt, where they can discern them at a greater distance. Unless a person has seen these dreadful conflagratinos, it is impossible to form the

the least idea of them. The flames that occupy generally an extent of several miles, are sometimes driven by the wind with such rapidity, that the inhabitants, even on horseback, have become a prey to them. The American sportsmen and the savages preserve themselves from this danger by a very ingenious method; they immediately set fire to the part of the meadow where they are, and then retire into the space that is burnt, where the flame that threatened them stops for the want of nourishment.

CHAP. XVII.

General observations upon Kentucky.—Nature of the soil.—First settlements in the state.—Right of property uncertain.—Population.

THE state of Kentucky is situated 36 deg. 30 min. and 39 deg. 30 min. north latitude, and 28 deg. and 89 deg. west longitude; its boundaries to the north-west are the Ohio, for an extent of about seven hundred and sixty miles, to the east of Virginia, and to the south of Tennessea; it is separated from Virginia by the river Sandy and the Laurel Mountains, one of the principal links of the Alleghanies. The greatest length of this state is about four hundred miles, and its greatest breadth about two hundred. This vast extent appears to lie upon a bank of chalky stone, identic in its nature, and covered with a stratum of vegetable earth, which varies in its composition, and is from ten to fifteen feet thick. The boundaries of this immense bank are not yet prescribed in any correct manner, but its thickness must be very considerable, to judge of it by the rivers in the country, the borders of which, and particularly those of the Kentucky and Dick rivers, which is one branch of it, rise, in some parts, three hundred feet perpendicular, where the chalky stone is seen quite bare.

The soil in Kentucky, although irregular, is not mountainous, if we except some parts contiguous to the Ohio and on this side Virginia. The chalky stone, and abundant coal mines which lie useless, are the only mineral substances worthy of notice. Iron mines are very scarce there, and, to the best of my remembrance, but one was worked, which is far from being sufficient for the wants of the country.

The Kentucky and Green rivers empty themselves into the Ohio, after a course of three hundred miles; they fall so low in summer time, that they are forded a hundred and fifty miles from their *embouchure*; but in the winter and spring they experience such sudden and strong increases that the waters of the Kentucky rise about forty feet in four-and-twenty hours. This variation is still more remarkable in the secondary rivers which run into it; the latter, though frequently from ten to fifteen fathoms broad, preserve such little water in summer, that there is scarcely one of them which cannot be crossed without wetting the feet; and the stream of water that serpentines upon the bed of chalky rock is at that time reduced to a few inches in depth; in consequence of which we may look upon the Kentucky as an immense bason, which, independent of the natural illapse of its waters through the channel of the rivers, loses a great part of them by interior openings.

The Atlantic part of the United States in that respect affords a perfect constrast with Kentucky, as on the other side of the Alleghanies not the least vestige of chalky stone is seen. The rivers, great and small, however distant from their source, are subject to no other change in the volume of their waters but what results from a more or less rainy season; and their springs, which are very numerous, always supply water in abundance; this applies more particularly to the southern states, with which I am perfectly acquainted.

According to the succinct idea that we have just given of Kentucky, it is easy to judge that the inhabitants are exposed to a very serious inconvenience, that of wanting water in the summer; still we must except those in the vicinity of great rivers and their principal channels, that always preserve water enough to supply their domestic wants; thence it results that many estates, even among the most fertile, are not cleared, and that the owners cannot get rid of them without the greatest difficulty, as the emigrants, better informed now a days, make no purchases before they have a correct statement of localities.

Kentucky is that of the three states situated west of the Alleghanies which was first populated. This country was discovered in 1770, by some Virginia sportsmen, when the favourable accounts they gave of it induced others to go there. No fixed establishment, however, was formed there before 1780. At that time this immense country was not occupied by any Indian nation; they went there to hunt, but all with one common assent made a war of extermination against those who wished to settle there. Thence this country derives the name of Kentucky, which signifies, in the language of the natives, *the Land of Blood.* When the whites made their appearance there, the natives showed still more opposition to their establishment; they carried for a long time death and desolation, and dispatched, after their usual mode, their prisoners in the most cruel torments. This state of things lasted till 1783, at which time the American population having become too strong for them to penetrate to the centre of the establishment, they were reduced to the necessity of attacking the emigrants on their route; and, on the other hand, they were deserted by the English in Canada, who had abetted and supported them in the war.

In 1782 they began to open roads for carriages in the interior of the country; prior to this there were only paths practicable for persons on foot and horseback. Till 1788 those who emigrated from the eastern states travelled by way of Virginia. In the first place, they went to Block House, situated in Holston, westward of the mountains; and as the government of the United States did not furnish them with an escort, they waited at this place till they were sufficiently numerous to pass in safety through the Wilderness, an uninhabited space of a hundred and thirty miles, which they had to travel over before they arrived at Crab Orchard, the first post occupied by the whites. The enthusiasm for emigrating to Kentucky was at that time carried to such a degree in the United States, that some years upwards of twenty thousand have been known to pass, and many of them had even deserted their estates, not having been able to dispose of them quick enough. This overflow of new colonists very soon raised the price of land in Kentucky, from two-pence and two-pence halfpenny per acre, it suddenly rose to seven or eight shillings. The stock-jobbers profited by this infatuation, and, not content with a moderate share of gain, practised the most illegal measures to dispose of the land to great advantage. They went so far as to fabricate false plans, in which they traced rivers favourable for mills and other uses; in this manner many ideal lots, from five hundred to a hundred thousand acres, were sold in Europe, and even in several great towns of the United States.

Till the year 1792, Kentucky formed a part of Virginia; but the distance from Richmond, the seat of government belonging to this state, being seven hundred miles from Lexinton, occasions the most serious inconveniences to the inhabitants, and their number rising considerably above that required to form an independent state, they were admitted into the union in the month of March following. The state of Virginia, on giving up its pretensions to that country, consented to it only on certain conditions; it imposed on the convention at Kentucky an obligation to follow, in part, its code of laws, and particularly to keep up the slave-trade.

Prior to the year 1782, the number of inhabitants at Kentucky did not exceed three thousand; it was about a hundred thousand in 1790, and in the general verification made in 1800, it amounted to two hundred thousand. When I was at Lexinton in the month of August 1802, its population was estimated at two hundred thousand, including twenty thousand negro slaves. Thus, in this state, where there were not ten individuals at the age of twenty-five who were born there, the number of the inhabitants is now as considerable as in seven of the old states; and there are only four where the population is twice as numerous. This increase, already so rapid, would have been much more so had it not been for a particular circumstance that prevents emigrants from going there; I mean the difficulty of proving the right of property. Of all the states in the union it is that wherein the rights of an individual are most subject to contest. I did not stop at the house of one inhabitant who was persuaded of the validity of his own right but what seemed dubious of his neighbour's.

Among the numerous causes which have produced this incredible confusion with respect to property, one of the principal may be attributed to the ignorance of the surveyors, or rather to the difficulty they experienced, in the early stage of things, in following their professions. The continual state of war in which this country was at that time obliged them frequently to suspend their business, in order to avoid being shot by the natives, who were watching for them in the woods. The danger they ran was extreme, as it is well known a native will go upwards of a hundred miles to kill a single enemy; he stays for several days in the hollow of a tree to take him by surprise, and when he has killed him, he scalps him, and returns with the same rapidity. From this state of things, the result was that the same lot has not only been measured several times by different surveyors, but more frequently it has been crossed by different lines, which distinguish particular parts of that lot from the lots adjacent, which, in return, are in the same situation with regard to those that are contiguous to them; in short, there are lots of a thousand acres where a hundred of them are not reclaimed. Military rights are still looked upon as the most assured. One very remarkable thing is, that many of the inhabitants find a guarantee for their estates that are thus confused; as the law, being always on the side of agriculture, enacts that all improvements shall be reimbursed by the person who comes forward to declare himself the first possessor; and as the estimation, on account of the high price of labour, is always made in favour of the cultivators, it follows that many people dare not claim their rights through fear of considerable indemnifications being awarded against them, and of being in return expelled by others, who might attack them at the moment when they least expected it. This incertitude in the right of property is an inexhaustible source of tedious and expensive law-suits, which serve to enrich the professional gentlemen of the country.

CHAP. XVIII.

Distinction of Estates.—Species of Trees peculiar to each of them.—Ginseng.—Animals in Kentucky.

IN Kentucky, as well as in Pennsylvania, Virginia and Carolina, the estates are divided into three classes, for the better assessment of the taxes. This division with respect to the fertility of the land is relative to each of these states; thus in Kentucky, for example, they would put in the second class estates, which, east of the mountains, would be ranked in the first, and in the third, those which in Georgia and Low Carolina would be the second. I do not mean, however, to say by this that there are not some possessions in the eastern states as fertile as in the western; but they are seldom found except along the rivers and in the vallies, and do not embrace so considerable a tract of country as in

Kentucky, and that part of Tennessea situate west of the Cumberland Mountains.

In these two states they appreciate the fertility of the land by the different species of trees that grow there; thus when they announce the sale of an estate, they take care to specify the particular species of trees peculiar to its various parts, which is a sufficient index for the purchaser. This rule, however, suffers an exception to the Barrens, the soil of which, as I have remarked, is fertile enough, and where there are notwithstanding here and there Scroby oaks, or *quercus nigra*, shell-barked hickeries, or *juglans hickery*, which in forests characterise the worst of soil. In support of this mode of appreciating in America the fecundity of the soil by the nature of the trees it produces, I shall impart a remarkable observation that I made on my entering this-state. In Kentucky and Cumberland *, independent of a few trees natives of this part of these countries, the mass of the forests, in estates of the first class, is composed of the same species which

* In the United States they give the name of Cumberland to that part of Tennessea situated to the west of the mountains of the same name.

are found, but very rarely, east of the mountains, in the most fertile soil; these species are the following, *cerasus Virginia*, or cherry-tree; *juglans oblonga*, or white walnut; *pavia lutea*, buck-eye; *fraximus alba, nigra, cerulea*, or white, black, and blue ash; *celtis foliis villosis*, or ack berry; *ulmus viscosa*, or slippery elm; *quercus imbricaria*, or black-jack oak; *guilandina disica*, or coffee tree; *gleditsia triacanthos*, or honey locust; and the *annona triloba*, or papaw, which grows thirty feet in height. These three latter species denote the richest lands. In the cool and mountainous parts, and along the rivers where the banks are not very steep, we observed again the *quercus macrocarpa*, or over-cup white oak, the acorns of which are as large as a hen's egg; the *acer sacharinum*, or sugar-maple; the *fagus sylvatica*, or beech; together with the *planus occidentalis*, or plane: the *liriodendrum tulipifera*, or white and yellow poplar; and the *magnolia acuminata*, or cucumber-tree, all three of which measure from eighteen to twenty feet in circumference; the plane, as I have before observed, attains a greater diameter. The two species of poplar, i. e. the white and yellow wood, have not the least external character, neither in their leaves nor flowers, by which they may be distinguished from each other; and as the species of the yellow wood is of a much greater use, before they fell a tree they satisfy themselves by a notch that it is of that species.

In estates of the second class are the *fagus castanea*, or chesnut tree; *quercus rubra*, or red oak; *quercus tinctoria*, or black oak; *laurus sassafras*, or sassafras; *diospiros virginia*, or persimon; *liquidambar styraciflua*, or sweet gum; *nyssa villosa*, or gum tree, a tree which, in direct opposition to its name, affords neither gum nor resin. Those of the third class, which commonly are dry and mountainous, produce very little except black and red oaks, chesnut oaks of the mountains, *quercus prinus montana*, or rocky oak pines, and a few Virginia cedars.

The *juglans pacane* is found beyond the *embouchure* of the rivers Cumberland and Tennessea, whence they sometimes bring it to the markets at Lexinton. This tree does not grow east of the Alleghany Mountains. The *lobelia cardinalis* grows abundantly in all the cool and marshy places, as well as the *lobelia sphilitica*. The latter is more common in Kentucky than in the other parts of the United States that I travelled over. The *laurus bensoin*, or spice wood, is also very numerous there. The two kinds of *vaccinium* and *andromeda*, which form a series of more than thirty species, all very abundant in the eastern states, seem in some measure excluded from those of the western and the chalky region, where we found none, but the *andromeda arborea*.

In all the fertile parts covered by the forests the soil is completely barren; no kind of herbage is seen except a few plants, scattered here and there; and the trees are always far enough apart that a stag may be seen a hundred or a hundred and fifty fathoms off. Prior to the Europeans settling, the whole of this space, now bare, was covered with a species of the great articulated reed, called *arundinaria macrosperma*, or cane, which is in the woods from three to four inches diameter, and grows seven or eight feet high; but in the swamps and marshes that border the Mississippi it is upward of twenty feet. Although it often freezes in Kentucky, from five to six degrees, for several days together, its foliage keeps always green, and does not appear to suffer by the cold.

Although the ginseng is not a plant peculiar to Kentucky, it is still very numerous there. This induces me to speak of it here. The ginseng is found in America from Lower Canada as far as the state of Georgia, which comprises an extent of more than fifteen hundred miles. It grows chiefly in the mountainous regions of the Alleghanies, and is by far more abundant as the chain of these mountains incline south west. It is also found in the environs of New York and Philadelphia, as well as in that part of the northern states situated between the mountains and the sea. It grows upon the declivity of the hills, in the cool and shady places, where the soil is richest. A man cannot pull up above eight or nine pounds of fresh roots per day. These roots are always less than an inch diameter, even after fifteen years' growth, if by any means we can judge of it with certitude by the number of impressions that are to be seen round the upper part of the neck of the root, produced by the stalks that succeed each other annually. The shape of these roots is generally elliptical; and whenever it is biforked, which is very rare, one of the divisions is always thicker and longer than the other. The seeds of the ginseng are of a brilliant red, and fastened to each other. Every foot seldom yields more than two or three. They are very similar in shape and size to the wild honey suckle. When they are disencumbered of the substance that envelopes them they are flat and semicircular. Their taste is more spicy, and not so bitter as the root. A month or two after they are gathered they grow oily; and it is probable to the rancidity which in course of time the seed attains we must attribute the difficulty there is in rearing them when they are kept too long. They are full ripe from the 15th of September to the 1st of October. I gathered about half an ounce of them, which was a great deal, considering the difficulty there is in procuring them.

It was a French missionary who first discovered the ginseng in Canada. When it was verified, that this plant was the same as that which grows in Tartary, the root of which has such valuable qualities in the eyes of the Chinese, it became an article of trade with China. For some time after its discovery the root was sold for its weight in gold; but this lucrative trade was but of short duration. The ginseng exported from America was so badly prepared, that it fell very low in price, and the trade almost entirely ceased. However, for some time past it has been rather better. Though the Americans have been so long deprived of this beneficial trade, it can only be attributed to the want of precaution that they used either in the gathering or preparation of the ginseng. In Chinese Tartary this gathering belongs exclusively to the emperor; it is done only by his orders, and they proceed in it with the greatest care. It commences in autumn, and continues all the winter, the epoch when the root has acquired its full degree of maturity and perfection; and by the means of a very simple process they render it almost transparent.

In the United States, on the contrary, they begin gathering of ginseng in the spring, and end at the decline of autumn. Its root, then soft and watery, wrinkles in drying, terminates in being extremely hard, and loses thus a third of its bulk, and nearly half its weight. These causes have contributed in lowering its value. It is only gathered in America by the inhabitants whose usual occupations afford them leisure, and by the sportsmen, who, with their carabine, provide themselves, for this purpose, with a bag and a pickaxe. The merchants settled in the interior of the country purchase dried ginseng at the rate of ten pence per pound, and sell it again from eighteen pence to two shillings, at the seaports. I havenever heard particularly what quantity of it was exported annually to China, but I think it must exceed twenty-five to thirty thousand pounds weight. Within these four or five years this trade has been very brisk. Several persons begin even to employ the means made use of by the Chinese to make the root transparent. This process, long since described in several works, is still a secret which is sold for four hundred dollars in Kentucky. The ginseng thus prepared is purchased at six or seven dollars per pound, by the merchants at Philadelphia, and is, they say, sold again at Canton for fifty or a hundred, according to the quality of the roots. Again, the profits must be very considerable, since there are people who export it themselves from Kentucky to China.

They have again, in Kentucky, and the western country, the same animals that inhabit those parts east of the mountains, and even Canada: but a short time after the settling of the Europeans several species of them wholly disappeared, particularly the elks and bisons. The latter, notwithstanding, were more common there than in any other part of North America. The non-occupation of the country, the quantity of rushes and wild peas, which supplied them abundantly with food the whole year round; and the licks (places impregnated with salt, as I have before mentioned) are the causes that kept them there. Their number was at that time so considerable, that they were met in flocks of a hundred and fifty to two hundred. They were so far from being ferocious, that they did not fear the approach of the huntsmen, who sometimes shot them solely for the sake of having their tongue, which they looked upon as a delicious morsel. At four years old they weigh from twelve to fourteen hundred weight; and their flesh, it is said, is preferable to that of the ox. At present there are scarcely any from Ohio to the river Illinois. They have nearly deserted these parts, and strayed to the right bank of the Mississippi.

The only species of animals that are still common in the country are the following, viz. the deer, bear, wolf, red and grey fox, wild cat, racoon, opossum, and three or four kinds of squirrels.

The animal to which the Americans give the name of wild cat is the Canadian lynx, or simply a different species; and it is through mistake that several authors have advanced that the true wild cat, as they look upon to be the original of the domestic species, either existed in the United States, or more northerly.

The racoon, or *ursus lotor*, is about the size of a

fox, but not so tall and more robust. Taken young, it very soon grows tame, and stays in the house, where it catches mice similar to a cat. The name of *lotor* is very appropriate, as the animal retires in preference in the hollow trees that grow by the side of creeks or small rivers that run through the swamp; and in these sorts of marshes it is most generally found. It is most common in the southern and western states, as well as in the remote parts of Pennsylvania and Virginia. It is very destructive in the corn fields. The usual method of catching this animal is with dogs, in the dead of the night, as it is very rarely to be seen in the day time. Its skin is very much esteemed, throughout the United States, by the hat manufacturers, who purchase them at the rate of two shillings each.

Nearer toward the houses the inhabitants are infested with squirrels, which do also considerable damage to the corn. This species *sciurus coroliniamus*, is of a greyish colour, and rather larger than those in Europe. The number of them is so immense, that several times a day the children are sent round the fields to frighten them away. At the least noise they run out by dozens, and take shelter upon the trees, whence they come down the very moment after.

As well as the bears in North America, they are subject to emigrations. Toward the approach of winter they appear in so great a number, that the inhabitants are obliged to meet together in order to destroy them. An excursion for this purpose, every now and then, is looked upon as pleasure. They go generally two by two, and kill sometimes thirty or forty in a morning. A single man, on the contrary, could scarcely kill one, as the squirrel, springing upon the branch of a tree, keeps turning round successively to put himself in opposition to the gunner. I was at one of these sporting parties, where, for dinner, which is generally taken in some part of the wood appointed for the rendezvous; they had above sixty of them roasted. Their flesh is white and exceedingly tender, and this method of dressing them is preferable to any other.

Wild turkies, which begin to grow very scarce in the southern states, are still extremely numerous in the west. In the parts least inhabited they are so very tame, that they may be shot with a pistol. In the east, on the contrary, and more particularly in the environs of the sea-ports, it is very difficult to approach them. They are not alarmed at a noise, but they have a very piercing sight, and as soon as they perceive the gunner they fly with such swiftness that it is impossible for a dog to overtake them for several minutes; and when they see themselves on the point of being taken, they escape by resuming their flight. Wild turkies usually frequent the swamps and the sides of creeks and rivers, whence they only go out morning and evening. They perch upon the tops of the loftiest trees, where, notwithstanding their size, it is not always easy to perceive them. When they are not frightened, they return upon the same trees for several weeks together.

For the space of eight hundred leagues east of Mississippi there is only this one species of the wild turkey. They are much larger than those that we have in our farm-yards. In autumn and winter they chiefly feed on chesnuts and acorns. At that time some are shot that weigh from thirty to forty pounds. The variety of domestic turkies proceeds originally from this species of wild turkies; and when it has not been crossed with the common species, it preserves the primitive colour of its plumage, and that of the feet, which are of a deep red. Though ever since the year 1525 our domestic turkies were naturalized in Spain, whence they were introduced into Europe, it is probable that they are natives of some of the more southern parts of America, where there may be, I have no doubt, a different species from that found in the United States.

CHAP. XIX.

Different kinds of culture in Kentucky.—Exportation of colonial produce.—Peach trees.—Taxes.

IN the state of Kentucky, like those of the southern parts, nearly the whole of the inhabitants, isolated in the woods, cultivate their estates themselves, and particularly in harvest time they assist each other; while some, more independent, have their land cultivated by negro slaves.

They cultivate, in this state, tobacco, hemp, and different sorts of grain from Europe, principally wheat and Indian corn. The frosts, which begin very early, are unfavourable to the culture of cotton, which might be a profitable part of their commerce, provided the inhabitants had any hopes of success. It is by the culture of Indian corn that all those who form establishments commence; since for the few years after the ground is cleared the soil is so fertile in estates of the first class, that the corn drops before it ears. Their process in husbandry is thus: after having opened, with the plough, furrows about three feet from each other, they cut them transversely by others at an equal distance, and set seven or eight grains in the points of intersection. When they have all come up, only two or three plants are left in the ground; a necessary precaution, in order to give free scope for the vegetation, and to insure a more abundant harvest. Toward the middle of the summer the leaves from the bottom of the stalk begin to wither, and successively those from the top. In proportion as they dry up they are carried away carefully, and reserved as a winter sustenance for horses, which prefer that kind of forage to the best hay.

In estates of the first class, that yield annually, Indian corn grows from ten to twelve feet high, and produces, in a common year, forty to fifty English bushels per acre, and sixty to seventy five in abundant years. Some have been known, the second and third year after the land has been cleared, to yield a hundred. The bushel, weighing about fifty to fifty-five pounds, never sells for more than a quarter of a dollar, and sometimes does not bring half the money.

The species of corn that they cultivate is long and flat in point of shape, and generally of a deep yellow. The time of harvest is toward the end of September. A single individual may cultivate eight or ten acres of it. The culture of corn is one of the most important of the country; much more, however, with regard to exportation than as an object of consumption. The county of Fayette, of which Lexinton is the chief town, and the surrounding counties, are those that supply the most. Good estates produce from twenty-five to thirty bushels per acre, weighing about sixty pounds, although they never manure the ground, nor till it more than once.

The harvest is made in the commencement of July. The corn is cut with a sickle, and threshed the same as in other parts of Europe. The corn is of a beautiful colour, and I am convinced, through the excellence of the soil, that the flour will be of a superior quality to that of Philadelphia, which, as it is well known, surpasses in whiteness the best that grows in France.

The plough which they make use of is light,

without wheels, and drawn by horses. It is the same in all the southern states.

The blight, the blue flower, and the poppy, so common in our fields among the corn, have not shewn themselves in North America.

The harvest of 1802 was so plentiful in Kentucky, that in the month of August, the time that I was at Lexinton, corn did not bring more than eighteen pence per bushel, (about two shillings per hundred weight). It had never been known at so low a price. Still this fall was not only attributed to the abundance of the harvest, but also on account of the return of peace in Europe. They are convinced, in the country, that at this price the culture of corn cannot support itself as an object of commerce; and that in order for the inhabitants to cover their expense the barrel of flour ought not to be sold at New Orleans for less than four or five dollars.

In all the United States the flour that they export is put into slight barrels made of oak, and of an uniform size. In Kentucky the price of them is about three-eighths of a dollar, (fifteen pence). They ought to contain ninety-six pounds of flour, which takes five bushels of corn, including the expenses of grinding.

The freightage of a boat to convey the flour to Low Louisiana costs about a hundred dollars. They contain from two hundred and fifty to three hundred barrels, and are navigated by five men, of whom the chief receives a hundred dollars for the voyage, and the others fifty each. They take, from Louisville, where nearly the whole embarkations are made, from thirty to thirty-five days to go to New Orleans. They reckon it four hundred and thirty-five miles from Louisville to the *embouchure* of the Ohio, and about a thousand miles thence to New Orleans, which makes it, upon the whole, a passage of fourteen hundred and thirty-five miles; and these boats have to navigate upon the river a space of eight or nine hundred miles without meeting with any plantations. A part of the crew return to Lexinton by land, which is about eleven hundred miles, in forty or forty-five days. This journey is extremely unpleasant, and those who dread the fatigues of it return by sea. They embark at New Orleans for New York and Philadelphia, whence they return to Pittsburgh, and thence go down the Ohio as far as Kentucky.

An inspector belonging to the port of Louisville inserted in the Kentucky Gazette of the 6th of August 1802, that 85,570 barrels of flour, from the 1st of January to the 30th of June following, went out of that port to Low Louisiana. More than two thirds of this quantity may be considered as coming from the state of Kentucky, and the rest from Ohio and the settlements situated upon the rivers Monongahela and Alleghany. The spring and autumn are principally the seasons in which this exportation is made. It is almost null in summer, an epoch at which almost all the mills are stopped for the want of water. Rye and oats come up also extremely well in Kentucky. The rye is nearly all made use of in the distilling of whiskey, and the oats as food for horses, to which they give it frequently in little bunches from two to three pounds, without being threshed.

The culture of tobacco has been greatly extended within these few years. The temperature of the climate, and the extraordinary fertility of the soil gives, in that respect, to this state, a very great advantage over that of Virginia; in consequence of which tobacco and corn form the principal branch of its commerce. It exports annually several thousand hogsheads, from a thousand to twelve hundred pounds each. The price of it is from two to three dollars per hundred weight.

Hemp, both raw and manufactured, is also an article of exportation. In the same year, 1802, there has been sent out of the country, raw 42,048 pounds, and 2402 hundred weight, converted into cables and various sorts of cordage.

Many of the inhabitants cultivate flax. The women manufacture linen of it for their families, and exchange the surplus with the trades-people for articles imported from Europe. These linens, though coarse, are of a good quality; yet none but the inferior inhabitants use them, the others giving a preference to Irish linens, which comprise a considerable share of their commerce. Although whiter, they are not so good as our linens of Bretagne. The latter would have found a great sale in the western states, had it not been for yielding Louisiana; since it is now clearly demonstrated that the expense of conveying goods which go up the river again from New Orleans to Louisville is not so great as that from Philadelphia to Limestone.

Although the temperature of the climate in Kentucky and other western states is more favourable to the culture of fruit trees, these parts have not been populated long enough for them to be brought to any great perfection. Beside, the Americans are by no means so industrious or interested in this kind of culture as the European states. They have confined themselves, at present, to the planting of peach and apple trees.

The former are very numerous, and come to the greatest perfection. There are five or six species of them, some forward, and others late, of an oval form, and much larger than our garden peaches. All the peaches grow in the open field, and proceed from kernels without being either pruned or grafted. They shoot so vigorously, that at the age of four years they begin to bear. The major part of the inhabitants plant them round their houses, and others have great orchards of them planted crosswise. They turn the hogs there for two months before the fruit gets ripe. These animals search with avidity for the peaches that fall in great numbers, and crack the stones of them for the kernels.

The immense quantity of peaches which they gather are converted in brandy, of which there is a great consumption in the country, and the rest is exported. A few only of the inhabitants have stills; the others carry their peaches to them, and bring back a quantity of brandy proportionate to the number of peaches they carried, except a part that is left for the expense of distilling. Peach brandy sells for a dollar a gallon, which is equal to four English quarts.

In Kentucky the taxes are assessed in the following manner: they pay a sum equivalent to one shilling and eight-pènce for every white servant, sixpence halfpenny for every negro, three-pence for a horse, two shillings per hundred acres of land of the first class, cultivated or not, seventeen-pence per hundred of the second class, and sixpence halfpenny per hundred of the third class. Although these taxes are, as we must suppose, very moderate, and though nobody complains of them, still a great number of those taxable are much in arrears. This is what I perceived by the numerous advertisements of the collectors that I have seen pasted up in different parts of the town of Lexinton. Again, these delays are not peculiar to the state of Kentucky, as I have made the same remark in those of the east.

CHAP. XX.

Particulars relative to the manners of the inhabitants of Kentucky.—Horses and Cattle.—Necessity of giving them salt.—Wild Horses caught in the Plains of New Mexico.—Exportation of salt provisions.

FOR some time past the inhabitants of Kentucky have taken to the rearing and training horses; and by this lucrative branch of trade they derive considerable profit, on account of the superfluous quantity of Indian corn, oats, and other forage, of which they are deficient at New Orleans.

Of all the states belonging to the union, Virginia is said to have the finest coach and saddle-horses, and those they have in this country proceed originally from them, the greatest part of which was brought by the emigrants who came from Virginia to settle in this state. The number of horses, now very considerable, increases daily. Almost all the inhabitants employ themselves in training and meliorating the breed of these animals; and so great a degree of importance is attached to the melioration, that the owners of fine stallions charge from fifteen to twenty dollars for the covering of a mare. These stallions come from Virginia, and, as I have been told, some were at different times imported from England. The horses that proceed from them have slim legs, a well proportioned head, and are elegantly formed. With draught-horses it is quite different. The inhabitants pay no attention with respect to improving this breed; in consequence of which they are small, wretched in appearance, and similar to those made use of by the peasantry in France. They appeared to me still worse in Georgia and Upper Carolina. In short, I must say that throughout the United States there is not a single draught-horse that can be in any wise compared with the poorest race of horses that I have seen in England. This is an assertion which many Americans may probably not believe, but still it is correct.

Many individuals profess to treat sick horses, but none of them have any regular notions of the veterinary art; an art which would be so necessary in a breeding country, and which has, within these few years, acquired so high a degree of perfection in England and France.

In Kentucky, as well as in the southern states, the horses are generally fed with Indian corn. Its nutritive quality is esteemed double to that of oats; notwithstanding sometimes they are mixed together. In this state horses are not limited as to food. In most of the plantations the manger is filled with corn, they eat of it when they please, leave the stable to go to grass, and return at pleasure to feed on the Indian wheat. The stables are nothing but log-houses, where the light penetrates on all sides, the interval that separates the trunks of the trees with which they are constructed not being filled up with clay.

The southern states, and in particular South Carolina, are the principal places destined for the sale of Kentucky horses. They are taken there in droves of fifteen, twenty and thirty at a time, in the early part of winter, an epoch when the most business is transacted at Carolina, and when the drivers are in no fear of the yellow fever, of which the inhabitants of the interior have the greatest apprehension.

They usually take eighteen or twenty days to go from Lexinton to Charleston. This distance, which is about seven hundred miles, makes a difference of twenty-five or thirty per cent in the price of horses. A fine saddle-horse in Kentucky costs about a hundred and thirty to a hundred and forty dollars.

During my sojourn in this state I had an opportunity of seeing those wild horses that are caught in the plains of New Mexico, and which descend from those that the Spaniards introduced there formerly. To catch them they make use of tame horses that run much swifter, and with which they approach them near enough to halter them. They take them to New Orleans and Natches, where they fetch about fifty dollars. The crews belonging to the boats that return by land to Kentucky frequently purchase some of them. The two that I saw and made a trial of were roan coloured, of a middling size, the head large, and not proportionate with the neck, the limbs thick, and the mane rather full and handsome. These horses have a very unpleasant gait, are capricious, difficult to govern, and even frequently throw the rider and take flight.

The number of horned cattle is very considerable in Kentucky; those who deal in them purchase them lean, and drive them in droves of from two to three hundred to Virginia, along the river Potomack, where they sell them to graziers, who fatten them in order to supply the markets of Baltimore and Philadelphia. The price of a good milch cow is, at Kentucky, from ten to twelve dollars. The milk in a great measure comprises the chief sustenance of the inhabitants. The butter that is not consumed in the country is put into barrels, and exported by the river to the Carribbees.

They bring up very few sheep in these parts; for, although I went upwards of two hundred miles in this state, I saw them only in four plantations. Their flesh is not much esteemed, and their wool is of the same quality as that of the sheep in the eastern states. The most that I ever observed was in Rhode Island.

Of all domestic animals hogs are the most numerous; they are kept by all the inhabitants, several of them feed a hundred and fifty or two hundred. These animals never leave the woods, where they always find a sufficiency of food, especially in autumn and winter. They grow extremely wild, and generally go in herds. Whenever they are surprised, or attacked by a dog or any other animal, they either make their escape, or flock together in the form of a circle to defend themselves. They are of a bulky shape, middling size, and straight eared. Every inhabitant recognizes those that belong to him by the particular manner in which their ears are cut. They stray sometimes in the forests, and do not make their appearance again for several months; they accustom them, notwithstanding, to return every now and then to the plantation, by throwing them Indian corn once or twice a week. It is surprising that in so vast a country, covered with forests, so thinly populated, comparatively to its immense extent, and where there are so few destructive animals, pigs have not increased so far as to grow completely wild.

In all the western states, and even to the east of the Alleghanies, two hundred miles of the sea coast, they are obliged to give salt to the cattle. Were it not for that, the food they give them would never make them look well; in fact, they are so fond of it that they go of their own accord to implore it at the doors of the houses every week or ten days, and spend hours together in licking the trough into which they have scattered a small quantity for them. This want manifests itself most among the horses;

but it may be on account of their having it given them more frequently.

Salt provisions form another important article of the Kentucky trade. The quantity exported in the first six months of the year 1802 was seventy-two thousand barrels of dried pork, and two thousand four hundred and eighty-five of salt.

Notwithstanding the superfluity of corn that grows in this part of the country, there is scarcely any of the inhabitants that keep poultry. This branch of domestic economy would not increase their expense, but add a pleasing variety in their food. Two reasons may be assigned for this neglect; the first is, that the use of salt provisions, (a use to which the prevalence of the scurvy among them may be attributed,) renders these delicacies too insipid; the second, that the fields of Indian corn contiguous to the plantations would be exposed to considerable damage, the fences with which they are inclosed being only sufficient to prevent the cattle and pigs from trespassing.

The inhabitants of Kentucky, as we have before stated, are nearly all natives of Virginia, and particularly the remotest parts of that state; and exclusive of the gentlemen of the law, physicians, and a small number of citizens who have received an education suitable to their professions in the Atlantic states, they have preserved the manners of the Virginians. With them the passion for gaming and spirituous liquors is carried to excess, which frequently terminates in quarrels degrading to human nature. The public-houses are always crowded, more especially during the sittings of the courts of justice. Horses and law-suits comprise the usual topic of their conversation. If a traveller happens to pass by, his horse is appreciated; if he stops, he is presented with a glass of whiskey, and then asked a thousand questions, such as, Where do you come from? where are you going? what is your name? where do you live? what profession? were there any fevers in the different parts of the country you came through? These questions, which are frequently repeated in the course of a journey, become tedious, but it is easy to give a check to their inquiries by a little address; their only object being the gratification of that curiosity so natural to people who live isolated in the woods, and seldom see a stranger. They are never dictated by mistrust; for from whatever part of the globe a person comes, he may visit all the ports and principal towns of the United States, stay there as long as he pleases, and travel in any part of the country without ever being interrogated by a public officer.

The inhabitants of Kentucky eagerly recommend to strangers the country they inhabit as the best part of the United States, as that where the soil is most fertile, the climate most salubrious, and where all the inhabitants were brought through the love of liberty and independence! In the interior of their houses they are generally very neat; which induced me, whenever an opportunity offered, to prefer lodging in a private family rather than at a public house, where the accommodation is inferior, although the charges are considerably higher.

The women seldom assist in the labours of the field; they are very attentive to their domestic concerns, and the spinning of hemp or cotton, which they convert into linen for the use of their family. This employment alone is truly laborious, as there are few houses which contain less than four or five children.

Among the various sects that exist in Kentucky, those of the Methodists and Anabaptists are the most numerous. The spirit of religion has acquired a fresh degree of strength within these seven or eight years among the country inhabitants, since, independent of Sundays, which are scrupulously observed, they assemble, during the summer, in the course of the week, to hear sermons. These meetings, which frequently consist of two or three thousand persons who come from all parts of the country within fifteen or twenty miles, take place in the woods, and continue for several days. Each brings his provisions, and spends the night round a fire. The clergymen are very vehement in their discourses. Often in the midst of the sermons the heads are lifted up, the imaginations exalted, and the inspired fall backwards, exclaiming, "Glory! glory!" This species of infatuation happens chiefly among the women, who are carried out of the crowd, and put under a tree, where they lie a long time extended, heaving the most lamentable sighs.

There have been instances of two or three hundred of the congregation being thus affected during the performance of divine service; so that one-third of the hearers were engaged in recovering the rest. Whilst I was at Lexinton I was present at one of these meetings. The better informed people do not share the opinion of the multitude with regard to this state of ecstacy, and on this account they are branded with the appellation of *bad folks*. Except during the continuance of this preaching, religion is very seldom the topic of conversation. Although divided into several sects, they live in the greatest harmony; and whenever there is an alliance between the families, the difference of religion is never considered as an obstacle; the husband and wife pursue whatever kind of worship they like best, and their children, when they grow up, do just the same, without the interference of their parents.

Throughout the western country the children are kept punctually at school, where they learn reading, writing, and the elements of arithmetic. These schools are supported at the expense of the inhabitants, who send for masters as soon as the population and their circumstances permit; in consequence of which it is very rare to find an American who does not know how to read and write. Upon the Ohio, and in the Barrens, where the settlements are farther apart, the inhabitants have not yet been able to procure this advantage, which is the object of solicitude in every family.

CHAP. XXI.

Nasheville.—Commercial details.—Settlement of the Natches.

NASHEVILLE, the principal and the oldest town in this part of Tennessea, is situate upon the river Cumberland, the borders of which, in this part, are formed by a mass of chalky stone upwards of sixty feet in height. Except seven or eight houses that are built of brick, the rest, to the number of about a hundred and twenty, are constructed of wood, and distributed upon a surface of twenty-five or thirty acres, where the rock appears almost bare in every part. They cannot procure water in the town without going a considerable way about to reach the banks of the river, or descending by a deep and dangerous path. When I was at Nasheville one of the inhabitants was endeavouring to pierce the rock, in order to make a well; but at that time he had only dug a few feet, on account of the stone being so amazingly hard.

This little town, although built upwards of fifteen years, contains no kind of manufactory or public establishment; but there is a printing-office which publishes a newspaper once a week. They have also began to found a college, which has been presented with several benefactions for its endowment, but this establishment was only in its infancy, having but seven or eight students and one professor.

The price of labour is higher in this town than at Lexinton, and the same disproportion exists between this price and that of provisions. There appeared to be from fifteen to twenty shops, which are supplied from Philadelphia and Baltimore, but they did not seem so well stocked as those at Lexinton, and the articles, though dearer, are of an inferior quality. The cause of their being so dear may be in some measure attributed to the expense of carriage, which is much greater on account of the amazing distance the boats destined for Tennessea have to go up the Ohio. In fact, after having passed by Limestone, the place where they unload for Kentucky, and which is four hundred and twenty miles from Pittsburgh, they have still to make a passage up the river of six hundred and nineteen miles to reach the mouth of the river Cumberland, and a hundred and eighty miles to arrive at Nasheville, which, in the whole, comprises a space of one thousand five hundred and twenty-one miles from Philadelphia, of which twelve hundred are by water. Some merchants get their goods also from New Orleans, whence the boats go up the Mississippi, the Ohio, and Cumberland. This last distance is about twelve hundred and forty-three miles; viz. a thousand miles from New Orleans to the *embouchure* of the Ohio, sixty-three miles from thence to Cumberland, and a hundred and eighty from this river to Nasheville.

There are very few cultivators who take upon themselves to export the produce of their labour, consisting chiefly of cotton; the major part of them sell it to the tradespeople at Nasheville, who send it by the river to New Orleans, where it is expedited to New York and Philadelphia, or exported direct to Europe. These tradesmen, like those of Lexinton, do not pay always in cash for the cotton they purchase, but make the cultivators take goods in exchange, which adds considerably to their profit. A great quantity of it is also sent by land to Kentucky, where each family is supplied with it to manufacture articles for their domestic wants.

When I was there in 1802 they made the first attempt to send cottons by the Ohio to Pittsburgh, in order to be thence conveyed to the remote parts of Pennsylvania. I met several barges laden with them near Marietta; they were going up the river with a staff, and making about twenty miles a day. Thus are the remotest parts of the western states united by commercial interests, of which cotton is the basis, and the Ohio the tie of communication, the results of which must give a high degree of prosperity to this part of Tennessea, and insure its inhabitants a signal advantage over those of the Ohio and Kentucky, the territorial produce of which is not of a nature to meet with a great sale in the country or the adjoining parts, and which they are obliged to send to New Orleans.

I had a letter from Dr. Brown, of Lexinton, for Mr. William Peter Anderson, a gentleman of the law at Nasheville, who received me in the most obliging manner; I am also indebted to him for the acquaintance of several other gentlemen; among others was a Mr. Fisk, of New England, president of the college, with whom I had the pleasure of travelling to Knoxville. The inhabitants are very engaging in their manners, and use but little ceremony.

On my arrival, I had scarcely alighted when several of them who were at the inn invited me to their plantations.

All the inhabitants of the western country who go by the river to New Orleans, return by land, pass through Nasheville, which is the first town beyond the Natches. The interval that separates them is about six hundred miles, and entirely uninhabited; which obliges them to carry their provisions on horseback to supply them on the road. It is true they have two or three little towns to cross, inhabited by the Chicasaws; but instead of recruiting their stock there, the natives themselves are so indifferently supplied, that travellers are obliged to be very cautious lest they should wish to share with them. Several persons who have been this road assured me, that for a space of four or five hundred miles beyond the Natches the country is very irregular, that the soil is very sandy, in some parts covered with pines, and not much adapted to any kind of culture; but that the borders of the river Tennessea are, on the contrary, very fertile, and even superior to the richest counties in Kentucky and Tennessea.

The settlement of the Natches, which is described by the name of the Mississippi Territory, daily acquires a fresh degree of prosperity, notwithstanding the unhealthiness of the climate, which is such that three-fourths of the inhabitants are eyery year exposed to intermittent fevers during the summer and autumn; nevertheless, the great profits derived from the cotton entice an immense number of foreigners into that part. The population now amounts to five thousand whites and three thousand negro slaves.

The road that leads to the Natches was only a path that serpentined through these boundless forests, but the federal government have just opened a road, which is on the point of being finished, and will be one of the finest in the United States, both on account of its breadth and the solidity of the bridges constructed over the small rivers that cut through it; to which advantages it will unite that of being shorter than the other by a hundred miles. Thus we may henceforth, on crossing the western country, go in a carriage from Boston to New Orleans, a distance of more than two thousand miles.

CHAP. XXII.

Departure for Knoxville.—Arrival at Fort Blount. —Remarks upon the drying up of the Rivers in the Summer.—Plantations on the Road.—Fertility of the Soil.—Excursions in a Canoe on the River Cumberland.

ON the 5th of September I set out from Nasheville for Knoxville, with Mr. Fisk, sent by the state of Tennessea to determine in a more correct manner, in concert with the commissaries of Virginia, the boundaries between the two states. We did not arrive till the 9th at Fort Blount, built upon the river Cumberland, about sixty miles from Nasheville; we stopped on the road with different friends of Mr. Fisk, among others, at the house of General Smith, one of the oldest inhabitants in the country, where he has resided sixteen or seventeen years. It is to him they are indebted for the best map of this state, which is found in the *Geographical Atlas*, published by Matthew Carey, bookseller, at Philadelphia. He confessed to me, notwithstanding, that this map, taken several years ago, was in many respects imperfect. The General has a beautiful plantation cultivated in Indian wheat and cotton; he has also a neat distillery for peach brandy, which he sells at five shillings per gallon. In his leisure hours he busies himself in chemistry. I have seen at his house English translations of the works of Lavoisier and Fourcroy.

We likewise saw, *en passant*, General Winchester, who was at a stone house that was building for him on the road; this mansion, considering the country, bore the external marks of grandeur; it consisted of four large rooms on the ground floor, one story, and a garret. The workmen employed to finish the inside came from Baltimore, a distance of nearly seven hundred miles. The stones are of a chalky nature; there are no others in all that part of Tennessea except round flints, which are found in the beds of some of the rivers which come originally from the mountainous region, whence they have been hurried by the force of the torrents. On the other hand there are so very few of the inhabitants that build in this manner, on account of the price of workmanship, masons being still scarcer than carpenters and joiners.

Not far from the General's house runs a river,

from forty to fifty feet wide, which we crossed dry-footed. Its banks in certain places are upwards of twenty-five feet high, the bottom of its bed is formed with flag stones, furrowed by small grooves, about three or four inches broad, and as many deep, through which the water flowed; but on the contrary the tide is so high in winter, that by means of a lock, they stop a sufficient quantity to turn a mill, situated more than thirty feet in height.

We had now passed several of these rivers that we could have strided over, but which, during the season, are crossed by means of ferry-boats.

A few miles from General Winchester's plantation, and at a short distance from the road, is situated a small town, founded within these few years, and to which they have given the name of Cairo, in memory of the taking of Cairo by the French.

Between Nasheville and Fort Blount the plantations, although always isolated in the woods, are nevertheless, upon the road, within two or three miles of each other. The inhabitants live in comfortable log houses; the major part keep negroes, and appear to live happy and in abundance. For the whole of this space the soil is but slightly undulated at times very even, and in general excellent; in consequence of which the forests look very beautiful. It is in particular, at *Dixon's Spring*, fifty miles from Nasheville, and a few miles on this side Major Dixon's, where I sojourned a day and a half, that we remarked this great fertility. We saw again in the environs a considerable mass of forests, filled with those canes or reeds I have before mentioned, and which grow so close to each other, that at the distance of ten or twelve feet a man could not be perceived was he concealed there. Their tufted foliage presents a mass of verdure that diverts the sight amid these still and gloomy forests. I have before remarked that, in proportion as new plantations are formed, these canes in a few years disappear, as the cattle prefer the leaves of them to any other kind of vegetables, and destroy them still more by breaking the body of the plant while browzing on the top of the stalks. The pigs contribute also to this destruction, by raking up the ground in order to search for the young roots.

Fort Blount was constructed about eighteen years ago, to protect the emigrants who came at that time to settle in Cumberland, against the attacks of the natives, who declared a perpetual war against them, in order to drive them out; but peace having been concluded with them, and the population being much increased, they have been reduced to the impossibility of doing them farther harm, and the Fort has been destroyed. There now exists on this spot a beautiful plantation, belonging to Captain William Samsoh, with whom Mr. Fisk usually resides. During the two days that we stopped at his house, I went in a canoe up the river Cumberland for several miles. This mode of reconnoitring the natural productions still more various upon the bank of the rivers, is preferable to any other, especially when the rivers are like the latter, bounded by enormous rocks, which are so very steep, that scarcely any person ventures to ascend their lofty heights. In these excursions I enriched my collections with several seeds of trees and plants peculiar to the country, and divers other objects of natural history.

CHAP. XXIII.

Departure from Fort Blount to West Point, through the Wilderness.—Botanical excursions upon Roaring River.—Description of its Banks.—Saline productions found there.—Indian Cherokees.—Arrival at Knoxville.

ON the 11th of September we went from Fort Blount to the house of a Mr. Blackborn, whose plantation, situated fifteen miles from this fortress, is the last that the whites possess on this side the line, that separates the territory of the United States from that of the Indian Cherokees. This line presents, as far as West Point upon the Clinch, a country uninhabited upward of eighty miles in breadth, to which they give the name of the *Wilderness*, and of which the mountains of Cumberland occupy a great part. As Mr. Fisk was obliged to go to the court of justice, which is held a few miles from thence in the county, of Jackson; we deferred crossing the Wilderness for a few days, and I profited by his absence to go and see Roaring River, one of the branches of the Cumberland. This river, from ten to fifteen fathoms broad, received its name from the confused noise that is heard a mile distant, and which is occasioned by falls of water produced by the sudden lapse of its bed, formed by large flat stones contiguous to each other. These falls, from six, eight, to ten feet high, are so near together, that several of them are to be seen within the space of fifty to a hundred fathoms. We observed in the middle of this river, great stones, from five to six feet in diameter, completely round, and of which nobody could form the least idea how they could have been conveyed there.

The right bank of Roaring River rises in some places from eighty to a hundred feet, and surmounted at this height by rocks that jet out fifteen or twenty feet, and which cover again thick beds of ferruginous *schiste*, situated horizontally. The flakes they consist of are so soft and brittle, that as soon as they are touched, they break off in pieces of a foot long, and fall into a kind of dust, which, in the course of time, imperceptibly undermines the rocks. Upon the flakes of *schiste* that are least exposed to the air and water, we observed a kind of white efflorescence, extremely thin, and very similar to snow.

There exists again upon the banks of this river, and in other parts of Cumberland, immense caverns, where there are masses of aluminous substances, within so small a degree of the purity necessary to be employed in dying, that the inhabitants not only go to fetch it for their own use, but export it to Kentucky. They cut it into pieces with an axe; but nobody is acquainted there with the process used on the *Old Continent* to prepare the different substances, as it is found in trade.

Large rivulets, after having serpentined in the forests, terminate their windings at the steep banks of this river, whence they fall murmuring into its bed, and form magnificent cascades several fathoms wide. The perpetual humidity that these cascades preserve in these places gives birth to a multitude of plants which grow in the midst of a thick moss, with which the rock is covered, and which forms the most beautiful verdant carpet.

All these circumstances give the borders of Roaring River a cool and pleasing aspect, which I had never witnessed before on the banks of other rivers. A charming variety of trees and shrubs are also seen there, which are to be met with no where else. We observed the *magnolia auriculata, macrophilla, cordata, acuminata,* and *tripetala*. The fruit of these trees, so remarkable for the beauty of their flowers and superb foliage, were in the highest perfection. I gathered a few seeds to multiply them in France, and to add to the embellishment of our gardens. These seeds grow rancid very soon. I endeavoured to remedy this inconvenience by putting them into fresh moss, which I renewed every fortnight till my return to Carolina, where I continued the same precautions till the epoch of my embarking for Europe. I have since had the satisfaction to see that my pains were not fruitless, and that I succeeded by this means in preserving their germinative faculty.

Major Russel, with whom I went to lodge after I had taken my leave of Mr. Blackborn, and where Mr. Fisk rejoined me, furnished us very obligingly with necessary provisions for the two days journey through the territory of the Cherokees. Notwithstanding the harmony that at present subsists between the whites and these Indians, it is always more prudent to travel five or six in a party. Nevertheless as we were at a considerable distance from the usual place of *rendezvous*, where the travellers put up, we resolved to set out alone, and we arrived happily at West Point. This country is exceedingly mountainous, we could not make above forty-five miles the first day, although we travelled till midnight. We encamped near a small river, where there was an abundance of grass; and after having made a fire we slept in our rugs, keeping watch alternately in order to guard our horses, and make them feed close by us for fear of the natives, who sometime steal them in spite of all the precaution a traveller can take, as their dexterity in that point exceeds all that a person can imagine. During this day's journey we saw nothing but wild turkies, thirty or forty in a flight.

The second day after our departure we met a party of eight or ten Indians, who were searching for grapes and chinquapins, a species of small chesnuts, superior in taste to those in Europe. As we had only twenty miles to go before we reached West Point, we gave them the remainder of our provisions, with which they were highly delighted. Bread is a great treat for them, their usual food consisting of nothing but venison and wild fowl.

The road that crosses this part of the Indian territory cuts through the mountains in Cumberland; it is as broad and commodious as those in the environs of Philadelphia, in consequence of the amazing number of emigrants that travel through it to go and settle in the western country. It is, notwithstanding, in some places very rugged, but nothing near so much as the one that leads from Strasburgh to Bedford in Pennsylvania. About forty miles from Nasheville we met an emigrant family in a carriage, followed by their negroes on foot, that had performed their journey without any accident. Little boards, painted black and nailed upon the trees every three miles, indicate to travellers the distance they have to go.

In this part of Tennessee the mass of the forests is composed of all the species of trees that belong more particularly to the mountainous regions of North America, such as oaks, maples, and nut trees. Pines abound in those parts where the soil is the worst. What appeared to me very extraordinary was, to find some parts of the woods, for the space of several miles, where all the pines that formed at least one fifth part of the other trees were dead since the preceding year, and still kept all their withered foliage. I was not able to learn the causes that produced this singular phenomenon. I only heard that the same thing happens every fifteen or twenty years.

At West Point is established a fort, pallisadoed round with trees, built upon a lofty eminence, at the conflux of the rivers Clinch and Holston. The fedral government maintain a company of soldiers there, the aim of which is to hold the Indians in respect, and at the same time to protect them against the inhabitants on the frontiers, whose illiberal proceedings excite them frequently to war. The objects of these insults were to drive them from their possessions; but the government has prevented this fruitless source of broils and wars, by declaring that all the possessions occupied by the Indians within the boundaries of the United States, comprise a part of their domains.

The following trait will give an idea of the ferocious disposition of some of these Americans on the frontiers. One of them belonging to the environs of Fort Blount, had lost one of his horses, which had strayed from his plantation and penetrated some distance into the Indian territory. About a fortnight after it was brought to him by two Cherokees; they were scarcely fifty yards from the house when the owner perceiving them, killed one upon the spot with his carabine; the other fled and carried the news to his fellow-countrymen. The murderer was thrown itoprison; but was afterwards released for the want of evidence, although he stood convicted in the eyes of every one. During the time he was in prison the Indians suspended their resentment, in hopes that the death of their fellow-countryman would be revenged; but scarcely were they informed that he was set at liberty when they killed a white, at more than a hundred and fifty miles from the place where the first murder had been committed. To the present moment we have never been able to make the Indians comprehend that punishment should only fall upon the guilty; they conceive that the murder of one or more of their people ought to be avenged by the death of an equal number of individuals belonging to the nation of that person who committed the deed. This is a custom they will not renounce, more especially if the person so murdered belongs to a distinguished family, as among the Creeks and Cherokees there exists a superior class to the common of the nation. These Indians are above the middling stature, well proportioned, and healthy in appearance, notwithstanding the long fasting they frequently endure in pursuit of animals, the flesh of which forms their chief subsistence. The carabine is the only weapon they make use of; they are very dexterous with it, and kill at a very great distance. The usual dress of the men consists of a shirt, *à l'Europène*, which hangs loose, and of a slip of blue cloth about half a yard in length, which serves them as breeches; they put it between their thighs, and fasten the two ends, before and behind, to a sort of girdle. They wear long gaiters, and shoes of stag skins prepared. When full dressed they wear a coat, waistcoat, and hat, but never any breeches. The natives of North America have never been able to adopt that part of our dress. They have only on the top of their heads a tuft of hair, of which they make several tresses, that hang down the sides of the face, and very frequently they attach quills or little silver tubes to the extremities. A great number of them pierce their noses, in order to put rings through, and cut holes in their ears, that hang down two or three inches, by the means of pieces of lead that they fasten to them when they are quite young. They paint their faces red, blue, or black.

A man's shirt and a short petticoat form the dress of the women, who wear also gaiters like the men; they let their hair grow, which is always of a jet black, to its natural length, but they never pierce their noses, nor disfigure their ears. In winter, the men and women, in order to guard against the cold, wrap themselves in a blue rug, which they always carry with them, and which forms an essential part of their luggage.

Near the fort is established a kind of warehouse where the Cherokees carry ginseng and furs, consisting chiefly of bear, stag, and otter skins. They give them in exchange for coarse stuffs, knives, hatchets, and other articles that they stand in need of.

I learnt at West Point, of several persons who make frequent journies among the Cherokees that within these few years they take to the cultivating of their possessions, and that they make a rapid progress. Some of them have good plantations, and even negro slaves. Several of the women spin and manufacture cotton stuffs. The federal government devotes annually a sum to supply them with instruments necessary for agriculture and different trades. Being pressed for time I could not penetrate farther into the interior of the country, as I had intended, and I did not profit by the letters of recommendation that Mr. W. P. Anderson had given me for that purpose to the garrison-officers in the fort.

They reckon thirty-five miles from West Point to Knoxville. About a mile from West Point we passed through Kingstown, composed of thirty or forty log houses; after that the road runs upwards of eighteen miles through a rugged and flinty soil, although covered with a kind of grass. The trees that occupy this extent grow within twenty or thirty yards of each other, which makes it seem as though this district changes from the appearance of a meadow to that of a forest. After this the soil grows better, and the plantations are not so far apart.

CHAP. XXIV.

Knoxville.—Commercial intelligence.—Trees that grow in the environs.—Converting some parts of the Meadows into Forests.—River Nolachuky.—Greensville.—Arrival at Jonesborough.

KNOXVILLE, the seat of government belonging to the state of Tennessea, is situate upon the river Holston, in this part nearly a hundred and fifty fathoms broad. The houses that compose it are about two hundred in number, and chiefly built of wood. Although founded eighteen or twenty years ago, this little town does not yet possess any kind of establishment or manufactory, except two or three tan yards. Trade, notwithstanding, is brisker here than at Nasheville. The shops, though very few in number, are in general better stocked. The tradespeople get their provisions by land from Philadelphia, Baltimore, and Richmond in Virginia; and they send in return, by the same way, the produce of the country, which they buy of the cultivators, or take in barter for their goods. Baltimore and Richmond are the towns with which this part of the country does most business. The price of conveyance from Baltimore is six or seven dollars per hundred weight. They reckon seven hundred miles from this town to Knoxville, six hundred and forty from Philadelphia, and four hundred and twenty from Richmond.

They send flour, cotton and lime to New Orleans by the river Tennessea; but this way is not so much frequented by the trade, the navigation of this river being very much encumbered in two different places by shallows interspersed with rocks. They reckon about six hundred miles from Knoxville to the *embouchure* of the Tennessea in the Ohio, and thirty-eight miles thence to that of the Ohio in the Mississippi.

We alighted at Knoxville at the house of one Haynes, the sign of the General Washington, the best inn in the town. Travellers and their horses are accommodated there at the rate of five shillings per day; though this is rather dear for a country where the situation is by no means favourable to the sale of provisions, which they are obliged to send to more remote parts. The reason of things being so dear proceeds from the desire of growing rich in a short time, a general desire in the United States, where every man who exercises a profession or art wishes to get a great deal by it, and does not content himself with a moderate profit, as they do in Europe.

There is a newspaper printed at Knoxville which comes out twice a week, and written and published by Mr. Roulstone, a fellow-countryman and friend of my travelling companion, Mr. Fisk. It is very remarkable that most of the emigrants from New England have an ascendancy over the others in point of morals, industry, and knowledge.

On the 17th of September I took leave of Mr. Fisk, and proceeded towards Jonesborough, about a hundred miles from Knoxville, and situate at the foot of the lofty mountains that separate North Carolina from the state of Tennessea. On leaving Knoxville the soil is uneven, stony and very indifferent, of which it is an easy thing to judge by the quantity of pines, or *pinus mitis*, that are in the forests. We also found there an abundance of Chinquapin oaks, or *quercus prinus Chinquapin*, that seldom grow above three feet high, some of which were that year so loaded with acorns that they were bent to the ground. The sorel-tree, or *andromeda arborea*, is also very common. This tree, that rises about forty feet in the mountains, would be one of the most splendid ornaments for our gardens, on account of its opening clusters of white flowers. Its leaves are very acid, and many of the inhabitants prefer them to shumac for dying cottons.

I crossed the river Holston at Macby, about fifteen miles from Knoxville; here the soil grows better, and the plantations are nearer together, although not immediately within sight of each other. At some distance from Macby the road, for the space of two miles, runs by the side of a copse, extremely full of young suckers, the highest of which was not above twenty feet. As I had never seen any part of a forest so composed before, I made an observation of it to the inhabitants of the country, who told me that this place was formerly part of a barren, or meadow, which had naturally clothed itself again with trees, that fifteen years since they had been totally destroyed by fire, in order to clear the land, which is a common practice in all the southern states. This example appears to demonstrate that the spacious meadows in Kentucky and Tennessea owe their birth to some great conflagration that has consumed the forests, and that they are kept up as meadows by the custom that is still practised of annually setting them on fire. In these conflagrations, when chance preserves any part from the ravages of the flame, for a certain number of years they are re-stocked with trees; but as it is then extremely thick, the fire burns them completely down, and reduces them again to a sort of meadow. We may thence conclude, that in these parts of the country the meadows encroach continually upon the forests. The same has probably taken place in Upper Louisiana and New Mexico, which are only immense plains, burnt annually by the natives, and where there is not a tree to be found.

I stopped the first day at a place where most of the inhabitants are Quakers, who came fifteen or eighteen years since from Pennsylvania. The one with whom I lodged had an excellent plantation, and his log-house was divided into two rooms, which is very uncommon in that part of the country. Around the house magnificent apple-trees were planted, which, although produced from pips, bore fruit of an extraordinary size and luxuriance in taste, which proves how well this country is adapted for the culture of fruit trees. Here, as well as in Kentucky, they give the preference to the peach, on account of their making brandy with it. At the same house where I stopped there were two emigrant families, forming together ten or twelve persons, who were going to settle in Tennessea. Their ragged clothes, and the miserable appearance of their children, who were bare-footed and in their shirts, was a plain indication of their poverty, a circumstance by no means uncommon in the United States. At the same time it is not in the western country that the riches of the inhabitants consist in specie; for I am persuaded that not one in ten of them are in possession of a single dollar; still each enjoys himself at home with the produce of his estate, and the money arising from the sale of a horse or a few cows is always more than sufficient to procure him the secondary articles that come from England.

The following day I passed by the iron-works, situate about thirty miles from Knoxville, where I stopped some time to get a sample of the native ore. The iron that proceeds from it they say is of an excellent quality. The road at this place divides into two branches, both of which lead to Jonesborough; but as I wanted to survey the banks of the river Nolachuky, so renowned in that part of the country for their fertility, I took the right, although it was rather longer, and not so much frequented. About six or seven miles from the iron-works we found upon the road small rock crystals, two or three inches long, and beautifully transparent. The facets of the pyramids that terminate the two extremities of the prism are perfectly equal with respect to size, they are loose, and disseminated in a reddish kind of earth, and rather clayey. In less than ten minutes I picked up forty. Arrived on the boundaries of the river Nolachuky, I did not observe any species of trees or plants that I had not seen elsewhere, except a few poplars and horse-chesnuts, which bore a yellow blossom. Some of these poplars were five or six feet in diameter, perfectly straight, and free from branches for thirty or forty feet from the earth.

On the 21st I arrived at Greenville, which contains scarcely forty houses, constructed with square beams something like the log-houses. They reckon twenty-five miles from this place to Jonesborough. In this space the country is slightly mountainous, the soil more adapted to the culture of corn than that of Indian wheat, and the plantations are situated upon the road, two or three miles distant from each other.

Jonesborough, the last town in Tennessea, is composed of about a hundred and fifty houses, built of wood, and disposed on both sides the road. Four or five respectable shops are established there, and the tradespeople who keep them have their goods from Richmond and Baltimore. All kinds of English-manufactured goods are as dear here as at Knoxville. A newspaper in folio is published at this town twice a week. Periodical sheets are the only works that have ever been printed in the towns or villages situate west of the Alleghanies.

CHAP. XXV.

General observations on the State of Tennessea.—Rivers Cumberland and Tennessea.—What is meant by East Tennessea or Holston, and West Tennessea or Cumberland.—First settlements in West Tennessea.—Trees natives of that country.

THE state of Tennessea is situated between 35 and 36 deg. 30 min. latitude, and 80 and 90 deg. 30 min. longitude. It is bounded north by Kentucky, south by the territories belonging to the Indian Cherokees and Chactaws, west by the Ohio, and east by the Alleghany Mountains, which separate it from Virginia and North Carolina. Its extent in breadth is nearly a hundred and three miles by three hundred and sixty in length. Prior to the year 1796, the epoch of its being admitted into the Union, this country comprised a part of North Carolina. The two principal rivers are the Cumberland and Tennessea, which flow into the Ohio eleven miles distant from each other, and are separated by the chain of mountains in Cumberland.

The river Cumberland, known to the French Canadians by the name of the river Shavanon, derives its source in Kentucky, amidst the mountains that separate it from Virginia. Its course is about four hundred and fifty miles. It is navigable, in winter and spring, for three hundred and fifty miles from its *embouchure*; but in summer, not above fifty miles from Nasheville. The river Tennessea, named by the French Canadians the Cherokee River, is the most considerable of all those that empty themselves into the Ohio. It begins at West Point, where it is formed by the junction of the rivers Clinch and Holston, which derive their source in that part of the Alleghany Mountains situated in Virginia, each of which are more than a hundred fathoms broad at their *embouchure*. Both are navigable to an immense distance, and particularly the Holston, which is so for two hundred miles. The river French Broad, one of the principal branches of the Holston, receives its waters from the Nolachuky, is about twenty fathoms broad, and is navigable in the spring. Thus the Tennessea, with the Holston, has, in the whole, a navigable course for near eight hundred miles: but this navigation is interrupted six months in the year by the muscle shoals, a kind of shallows interspersed with rocks, which are met with in its bed two hundred miles from its *embouchure* in the Ohio. From West Point the borders of this great river are yet almost entirely uninhabited. The signification of the name of Tennessea, which it bears, is unknown to the Cherokees and Chactaws that occupied this country before the whites. Mr. Fisk, who has had several conversations with these Indians, never heard any precise account; in consequence of which it is most likely that this name has been given to it by the nation that the Cherokees succeeded.

The Cumberland Mountains are but a continuation of Laurel Mountain, which itself is one of the principal links of the Alleghanies. These mountains, on the confines of Virginia, incline more toward the west, and by the direction which they take, cut obliquely in two the state of Tennessea, which, in consequence, divides East and West Tennessea into two parts, both primitively known by the names of the Holston and Cumberland settlements, and which afford each a different aspect, both by the nature of the country, and by the productions that grow there.

West Tennessea comprises two-thirds of this state. The greater part of it reposes upon a bank of chalky substance of the same nature, the beds of which are horizontal. The stratum of vegetable earth with which it is covered appears generally not so thick as in Kentucky, and participates less of the clayey nature. It is usually, in point of colour, of a dark brown, without the least mixture of stony substances. The forests that cover the country clearly indicate how favourable the soil is for vegetation, as most of the trees acquire a very large diameter. Iron mines are also as scarce there as in Kentucky; and provided any new ones were discovered, they would have been worked immediately, since the iron that is imported from Pennsylvania is at such an enormous price.

The secondary rivers which in this part of Tennessea run into Cumberland are almost completely dry during the summer; and it is probable enough, that when the population grows more numerous, and the plantations are formed farther from their banks, the want of water will be more severely felt in this part than in Kentucky. There are, notwithstanding, several large rivulets or creeks that issue from excavations that are found at the foot of the mountains, in different parts of the country: at the same time it has been remarked that these kind of sources never fail, although the water is not so deep in summer:

Just at the mouth of these subterraneous passages they are sometimes accompanied with a current of air strong enough to extinguish a light. I observed this particularly myself at the spring of the rivulet called Dixon's Spring, and of another situated about four miles from Nasheville.

It was in 1780 that the whites first made the attempt to travel over the Cumberland Mountains, and to settle in the environs of Nasheville; but the emigrants were not very numerous there till the year 1789. They had to support, for several years, a bloody war against the Indian Cherokees, and till 1795 the settlements at Holston and Kentucky communicated with those in Cumberland by caravans, for the sake of travelling in safety over so extensive a tract of uninhabited country that separated them; but for these five or six years past, since peace has been made with the natives, the communications formed between the countries are perfectly established; and although not much frequented, they travel there with as much safety as in any other part of the Atlantic states,

This country having been populated after that of Kentucky, every measure was taken at the commencement to avoid the great confusion that exists concerning the right of property in the latter state; at the same time the titles are looked upon as more valid, and not so subject to dispute. This reason, the extraordinary fertility of the soil, and a more healthy climate, are such great inducements to the emigrants of the Atlantic states, that most of them prefer settling in West Tennessea than in Kentucky. They reckon there, at present, thirty thousand inhabitants, and five or six thousand negro slaves.

With a few exceptions the various species of trees and shrubs that form the mass of the forests are the same as those that I observed in the most fertile parts of Kentucky. The *gleditsia triacanthos* is still more common there. Of this wood the Indians made their bows, before they adopted the use of fire-arms.

We found particularly, in these forests, a tree which, by the shape of its fruit and the disposition of its leaves, appears to have great affinity with the *sophora japonica*, the wood of which is used by the Chinese for dying yellow. My father, who discovered this tree in 1796, thought that it might be employed for the same use, and become an important object of traffic for the country. He imparted his conjectures to Mr. Blount, then governor of this state, and his letter was inserted in the Gazette at Knoxville on the 15th of March 1796. Several persons in the country having a great desire to know whether it were possible to fix the beautiful yellow which the wood of this tree communicated to the water by the simple infusion, cold, I profited by my stay at Nasheville to send twenty pounds of it to New York, the half of which was remitted to Dr. Mitchell, professor of chemistry, and the other addressed to Paris, to the Board of Agriculture, attached to the Minister of the Interior, in order to verify the degree of utility that might be derived from it. This tree very seldom rises above forty feet, and grows, in preference, on the knobs, species of little hills, where the soil is very rich. Several of the inhabitants have remarked that there is not in the country a single species of tree that produces so great an abundance of sap. The quantity that it supplies exceeds even that of the sugar maple, although the latter is twice its bulk. The epoch of my stay at Nasheville being that when the seeds of this tree were ripe, I gathered a small quantity of them, which I brought over with me, and which have all come up. Several of the plants are at the present moment ten or fifteen inches high. It is very probable that this tree may be reared in France, and that it will endure the cold of our winters, and more so, as, according to what I have been told, the winters are as severe in Tennessea as in any parts of France.

West Tennessea is not so salubrious as Holston and Kentucky. A warmer and damper climate is the cause of intermittent fevers being more common there. Emigrants, for the first year of their settling there, and even travellers, are, during that season, subject to an exanthemetic affection similar to the itch. This malady, with which I began to be attacked before I reached Fort Blount, yielded to a cooling regimen, and repeated bathings in the rivers Cumberland and Roaring. This disorder is very appropriately called in the country the Tennessean itch.

CHAP. XXVI.

Different kinds of produce of West Tennessea.—Domestic manufactories for cottons encouraged by the legislature of this state.—Mode of letting out estates by some of the emigrants.

WEST Tennessea, or Cumberland, being situated under a more southerly latitude than Kentucky, is particularly favourable to the growth of cotton; in consequence of which the inhabitants give themselves up almost entirely to it, and cultivate but little more corn, hemp, and tobacco than what is necessary for their own consumption.

The soil, which is fat and clayey, appears to be a recent dissolving of vegetable substances, and seems, till now, less adapted for the culture of corn than that of Indian wheat. The harvests of this grain are as plentiful as in Kentucky; the blades run up ten or twelve feet high; and the ears, which grow six or seven feet from the earth, are from nine to ten inches in length, and proportionate in size. It is cultivated in the same manner as in other parts of the western country.

The crows, which are a true plague in the Atlantic states, where they ravage, at three different periods, the fields of Indian wheat, which are obliged to be sown again as many times, have not yet made their appearance in Tennessea; but it is very probable that this visit is only deferred, as they do, annually, great damage in Kentucky.

I must also observe here that the grey European rats have not yet penetrated into Cumberland, though they are very numerous in other parts of the country, particularly in those settlements belonging to the whites.

The culture of cotton, infinitely more lucrative

than that of corn and tobacco, is, as before observed, the most adhered to in West Tennessea. There is scarcely a single emigrant but what begins to plant his estate with it the third year after his settling in the country. Those who have no negroes cultivate it with the plough, nearly in the same manner as Indian wheat, taking particular care to weed and throw new earth upon it several times in the course of the season. Others lay out their fields in parallel furrows, made with the hoe, from twelve to fifteen inches high. It is computed that one man, who employs himself with this alone, is sufficient to cultivate eight or nine acres, but not to gather in the harvest. A man and a woman, with two or three children, may, notwithstanding, cultivate four acres with the greatest ease, independent of the Indian wheat necessary for their subsistence; and calculating upon a harvest of three hundred and fifty pounds weight per acre, which is very moderate according to the extreme fertility of the soil, they will have, in four acres, a produce of fourteen hundred pounds of cotton. Valuing it at the rate of eighteen dollars per hundred weight, the lowest price to which it had fallen at the epoch of the last peace, when I was in the country, gives two hundred and fifty-two dollars; from which deducting forty dollars for the expenses of culture, they will have a net produce of two hundred and twelve dollars; while the same number of acres, planted with Indian wheat, or sown with corn, would only yield at the rate of fifty bushels per acre; and twenty-five bushels of corn, about fifty dollars, reckoning the Indian wheat at thirteen pence, and the corn at two shillings and two pence per bushel; under the supposition that they can sell it at that price, which is not always the case. This light sketch demonstrates with what facility a poor family may acquire speedily, in West Tennessea, a certain degree of independence, particularly after having been settled five or six years, as they procure the means of purchasing one or two negroes, and of annually increasing their number.

The species of cotton which they cultivate here is

somewhat more esteemed than that described by the name of green-seed cotton, in which there is a trifling distinction in point of colour.

The cottons that are manufactured in West Tennessea are exceedingly fine, and superior in quality to those I saw in the course of my travels. The legislature of this state, appreciating the advantage of encouraging this kind of industry, and of diminishing, by that means, the importation of English goods of the same nature, has given, for these two years past, a premium of ten dollars to the female inhabitant who, in every county, presents the best manufactured piece; for in this part, as well as in Kentucky, the higher circles wear, in summer time, as much from patriotism as from economy, dresses made of the cottons manufactured in the country. At the same time they are convinced that it is the only means of preserving the little specie that is in the country, and of preventing its going to England.

The price of the best land does not yet exceed five dollars per acre in the environs of Nasheville, and thirty or forty miles from the town they are not even worth three dollars. They can at that price purchase a plantation completely formed, composed of two to three hundred acres, of which fifteen to twenty are cleared, and a log-house. The taxes in this state are also not so high as in Kentucky.

Among the emigrants that arrive annually from the eastern country at Tennessea there are always some who have not the means of purchasing estates; still there is no difficulty in procuring them at a certain rent; for the speculators who possess many thousand acres are very happy to get tenants for their land, as it induces others to come and settle in the environs; since the speculation of estates in Kentucky and Tennessea is so profitable to the owners, who reside upon the spot, and who, on the arrival of the emigrants, know how to give directions in cultivation, which speedily enhances the value of their possessions.

The conditions imposed upon the renter are to clear and inclose eight or nine acres, to build a log-house, and to pay to the owner eight or ten bushels of Indian wheat for every acre cleared. These contracts are kept up for seven or eight years. The second year after the price of two hundred acres of land belonging to a new settlement of this kind increases nearly thirty per cent.; and this estate is purchased in preference by a new emigrant, who is sure of gathering corn enough for the supplies of his family and cattle.

In this state they are not so famed for rearing horses as in Kentucky; yet the greatest care is taken to improve their breed, by rearing them with those of the latter state, whence they send for the finest mare foals that can be procured.

Although this country abounds with saline springs, none are yet worked, as the scarcity of hands would render the salt dearer than what is imported from the salt-pits of St. Genevieve, which supply all Cumberland. It is sold at two dollars per bushel, about sixty pounds weight.

CHAP. XXVII.

East Tennessea, or Holston.—Agriculture.—Population.—Commerce.

EAST Tennessea, or Holston, is situated between the loftiest of the Alleghany and Cumberland Mountains. It comprises, in length, an extent of nearly a hundred and forty miles, and differs chiefly from West Tennessea in point of the earth's being not so chalky, and better watered by the small rivers issuing from the adjacent mountains, which cross it in every part. The best land is upon their borders. The remainder of the territory, almost everywhere interspersed with hills, is of a middling quality, and produces nothing but white, red, black, chincapin, and mountain oaks, &c. intermixed with pines ; and, as we have before observed, except the *quercus macrocarpa,* the rest never grow, even in the most fertile places.

Indian wheat forms here also one of the principal branches of agriculture ; but it very seldom comes up above seven or eight feet high, and a produce of thirty bushels per acre passes for an extraordinary harvest. The nature of the soil, somewhat gravelly, appears more adapted for the culture of wheat, rye, and oats ; in consequence of which it is more adhered to than in Cumberland. That of cotton is little noticed, on account of the cold weather, which sets in very early. One may judge, according to this, that Holston is in every point inferior in fertility to Cumberland and Kentucky.

To consume the superfluity of their corn the inhabitants rear a great number of cattle, which they take four or five hundred miles to the seaports belonging to the southern states. They lose very few of these animals by the way, although they have to cross several rivers, and travel through an uninterrupted forest, with this disadvantage, of the cattle being extremely wild.

This part of Tennessea began to be inhabited in 1775, and the population is so much increased, that there is now computed to be about seventy thousand inhabitants, including three or four thousand negro slaves. In 1787 they attempted to form themselves into an independent state, under the name of the Franklin State; but this project was abandoned. It is still very probable, and has already been in question, that East and West Tennessea will ultimately form two distinct states, which will each enlarge itself by a new addition of part of the territory belonging to the Cherokee Indians. The natives, it is true, will not hear the least mention of a cession being made, objecting that their tract of country is barely sufficient to furnish, by hunting, a subsistence for their families. However, sooner or later they will be obliged to yield. The division of Tennessea cannot be long before it takes place, whether under the consideration of convenience, or the enterprising disposition of the Americans. It is commanded, on the one hand, by the boundaries that Nature herself has prescribed between the two countries, in separating them by the Cumberland Mountains; and on the other, by their commerce, which is wholly different, since Cumberland carries on its trade by the Ohio and Mississippi, while Holston does most by land with the seaports belonging to the Atlantic states, and has very little to do with New Orleans by the river Tennessea, and scarcely any with Cumberland and Kentucky. Under this consideration, Holston is, of all parts in the United States that are now inhabited, the most unfavourably situated, being on every side circumscribed by considerable tracts of country that produce the same provisions, and which are either more fertile or nearer to the borders of the sea.

What has been said relative to the manners of the inhabitants of Kentucky will apply, in a great measure to Tennessea, since they come, as the former do, from North Carolina and Virginia: still the inhabitants of Tennessea do not yet enjoy that degree of independence which is remarked among those of Kentucky. They appear also not so religious, although, in the mean time, they are very strict observers of Sundays. We found but very few churches in Tennessea. Itinerant preachers wander, in summer, through the different countries, and preach in the woods, where the people collect together.

CHAP. XXVIII.

Departure from Jonesborough for Morganton in Norh Carolina.—Journey over Iron Mountains.—Sojourn on the mountains.—Journey over the Blue Ridges and Linneville Mountains.—Arrival at Morganton.

ON the 21st of September 1802 I set out from Jonesborough to cross the Alleghanies for North Carolina. About nine miles from Jonesborough the road divides into two branches, which unite again fifty-six miles beyond the mountains. The left, which is principally for carriages, cuts through Yellow Mountain, and the other through Iron

Mountain. I took the latter, as I had been informed it was much the shortest. I only made nineteen miles that day, and put up at one Cayerd's, at the Limestone Cow, where I arrived benumbed with cold by the thick fog that reigns almost habitually in the vallies of these enormous mountains.

Seven miles on this side Cayerd's plantation, the road, or rather the path, begins to be so little cut that one can scarce discern the track for plants of all kinds that cover the superficies of it; it is also encumbered by forests of *rhododendrum*, shrubs from eighteen to twenty feet in height, the branches of which, twisting and interwoven with each other, impede the traveller every moment, insomuch that he is obliged to use an axe to clear his way. The torrents that we had continually to cross added to the difficulty and danger of the journey, the horses being exposed to fall on account of the loose round flints, concealed by the ebullition of the waters with which the bottom of these torrents are filled.

I had the day following twenty-three miles to

make without meeting with the least kind of a plantation. After having made the most minute inquiry with regard to the path I had to take, I set out about eight o'clock in the morning from the Limestone Cow, and after a journey of three hours I reached the summit of the mountain, which I recognized by several trees with "*the road*" marked on each, and in the same direction to indicate the line of demarcation that separates the state of Tennessea from that of North Carolina. The distance from the Limestone Cow to the summit of the mountain is computed to be about two miles and a half, and three miles thence to the other side. The declivity of the two sides is very steep, insomuch that it is with great difficulty a person can sit upon his horse, and that half the time he is obliged to go on foot. Arrived at the bottom of the mountain, I had again, as the evening before, to cross through forests of *rhododendrum*, and a large torrent called Rocky Creek, the winding course of which cut the path in twelve or fifteen directions; every time I was obliged to alight, or go up the torrent by walking into the middle for the space of ten or fifteen fathoms, in order to regain on the other bank the continuation of the path, which is very rarely opposite, and of which the entrance was frequently concealed by tufts of grass or branches of trees, which have time to grow and extend their foliage, since whole months elapse without its being passed by travellers. At length I happily arrived at the end of my journey. I then perceived the imprudence I had committed in having exposed myself without a guide in a road so little frequented, and where a person every moment runs the risk of losing himself on account of the sub-divisions of the road, that ultimately disappear, and which it would be impossible to find again, unless by being perfectly acquainted with the localities and disposition of the country, where obstacle upon obstacle oppose the journey of the traveller, and whose situation would in a short time become very critical from the want of provisions.

On the 23d I made twenty-two miles through a

country bestrewed with mountains, but not so lofty as that which I had just passed over, and arrived at the house of one Davenport, the owner of a charming plantation upon Doe river, a torrent about forty feet in breadth, and which empties itself into the Nolachuky. I had learnt the evening before, of the person with whom I had lodged, that it was at Davenport's my father had resided, and that it was this man who served him as a guide across the mountains when on his travels to discover their productions. I was at that time very far from thinking that at the same time when this worthy man was entertaining me about his old travelling companion, I lost a beloved father, who died a victim of his zeal for the progress of natural history upon the coast of the island of Madagascar!

I staid a week at Davenport's, in order to rest myself after a journey of six hundred miles that I had just made, and during this interval I travelled over the Blue Ridges that encompass his plantation. On the 2d of October 1802 I set out on my journey again, and proceeded towards Morganton, a distance of thirty-five miles. About four miles from Doe river I re-passed the chain of the Blue Ridges. Its summit is obtained by a gentle declivity, which is much longer and more rapid on the eastern side, without being impracticable for carriages. The journey over this mountain is computed to be about four miles and a half.

About five miles from the Blue Ridges are the Linneville Mountains, not quite so lofty as the latter, but steeper, and more difficult to ascend. The road that cuts through them is encumbered westward with large, flat stones, which impede the traveller on his route. From the summit of these mountains, which is not overstocked with trees, we discovered an immense extent of mountainous country covered with forests, and at their base only three small places cleared, which form as many plantations, three or four miles distant from each other.

From the Linneville Mountains to Morganton it is computed to be twenty-five miles, where I arrived on the 5th of October. In this interval the country is slightly mountainous, and the soil extremely bad; at the same time we did not find more than four or five plantations on the road. About a mile on this side the town we crossed the northern arm of the river Catabaw, in this part nearly fifty fathoms broad, although the source of this river is only fifty miles. The rains that had fallen in the mountains had produced a sudden increase of water, and the master of the ferry-boat conceiving it would not last long, had not thought proper to re-establish his boat, so that I was obliged to ford. One of his children pointed out to me the different directions that I had to take in order to avoid the immense cavities under water.

CHAP. XXIX.

General observations upon this part of the Chain of the Alleghanies.—Salamander which is found in the torrents.—Bear hunting.

IN Pennsylvania and Virginia the Alleghanies present themselves under the form of parallel furrows, but varying in their length. They are mostly near together, and form narrow vallies; but sometimes the interval that separates them is from twenty to thirty miles in length; again these spaces are filled with a multitude of hills of a lesser elevation, confusedly scattered, and in no wise affecting the direction of the principal chains. On the confines of North Carolina and Tennessea the Alleghanies are, on the contrary, isolated mountains, and only contiguous by their base; they embrace also in diameter an extent of country less considerable, and which is not computed to be more than seventy miles. The furrow that bears more particularly the name of the Alleghany Ridge in Pennsylvania, and that of Blue Ridge in North Carolina, is the only one that, continuing uninterruptedly, divides the rivers that run into the Atlantic Ocean from those that swell the current of the Ohio. The height of this chain is still infinitely less than that of the neighbouring mountains. It is here that the Alleghanies, which cross the United States for the space of nine hundred miles, have the highest elevation. This is the opinion of most of the inhabitants, who, from the mountainous part of Pennsylvania and Virginia, have emigrated on the confines of North Carolina, and who know the respective heights of all these mountains. That of the first rank is called Grandfather Mountain, the next Iron Mountain, and thus in succession Yellow Mountain, Black Mountain, and Table Mountain, which are all situate upon the western rivers. On the top of Yellow Mountain, the only one that is not stocked with trees, all the abovementioned may be seen.

We may again remark, in support of the preceding observation, that from the 10th to the 20th of September the cold is so keenly felt upon the mountains that the inhabitants are obliged to make a fire, which is not the case upon any of those in Virginia, although they are situated more northerly by several degrees: and besides I have since seen in my father's notes that he had observed trees and shrubs upon the Yellow and Grandfather Mountains that he did not meet with again till he reached Low Canada.

As the only ideas given concerning the height of the Alleghanies are the result of observations taken in Virginia, we see, according to that short exposition, that we have but an inaccurate account; this induced me to point out the highest mountains where their true elevation might be ascertained. They are about three hundred and sixty miles from Charleston, in

South Carolina, and five hundred and fifty from Philadelphia.

The mineral kingdom is very little diversified in these mountains. The mines which have hitherto been found are chiefly those of iron. They are worked with success, and the iron which they derive from it is of an excellent quality.

In the mountainous parts of Pennsylvania and Virginia the land, frequently dry and flinty, is of an indifferent nature. Here, on the contrary, the soil far from being flinty, is perpetually moist, and very fertile. We may judge of it by the vegetable strength of the trees, among which we observed the red and black oak, the sugar-maple, the ash, the yellow-blossomed chesnut, or the *magnolia acuminata* and *auriculata*, and the common chesnut, which grows to a prodigious height. The side of these mountains that looks north is sometimes covered exclusively with the *kalmia latifolia*, or calico-tree, from twelve to fifteen feet high. They frequently occupy spaces of from two to three hundred acres, which at a distance affords the aspect of a charming meadow. It is well known that this shrub excels every other in point of blossom.

In the great woods the superficies of the soil is covered with a species of wild peas, that rises about three feet from the earth, and serves as excellent fodder for the cattle. They prefer this pasturage to any other, and whenever they are driven from it they pine away, or make their escape to get to it again.

These mountains begin to be populated rapidly. The salubrity of the air, the excellence of the water, and more especially the pasturage of these wild peas for the cattle, are so many causes that induce new inhabitants to settle there.

Estates of the first class are sold at the rate of two dollars, and the taxes are not more than a half-penny per acre. Indian corn, wheat, rye, oats, and peach trees, are the sole objects of culture.

In the torrents we found a species of salamander, called by the inhabitants the mountain alligator;

many of which are upwards of two feet in length. It was in Doe river that my father caught the one which is described in *The New Dictionary of Natural History*, published by Deterville.

The inhabitants of these mountains are famed for being excellent hunters. Towards the middle of autumn most of them go in pursuit of bears, of which they sell the skins, and the flesh, which is very good, serves them in a great measure for food during that season. They prefer it to all other kinds of meat, and look upon it as the only thing they can eat without being indisposed by it. They make also of their hind legs the most delicious hams. In autumn and winter the bears grow excessively fat; some of them weigh upward of four hundred weight. Their grease is consumed in the country instead of oil. They hunt them with great dogs, which, without going near them, bark, teaze, and oblige them to climb up a tree, when the hunter kills them with a carabine. A beautiful skin sells for a dollar and a half or two dollars. The black bear of North

America lives chiefly on roots, acorns and chesnuts. In order to procure a greater quantity of them, he gets up into the trees, and as his weight does not permit him to climb to any height, he breaks off the branch where he has observed the most fruit by hugging it with one of his fore paws. I have seen branches of such a diameter that these animals must be endowed with an uncommon strength to have been able to break them by setting about it in this manner. In the summer, when they are most exposed to want victuals, they fall upon pigs, and sometimes even upon men.

CHAP. XXX.

Morganton.—Departure for Charleston.—Lincolnton.— Chester.—Winesborough.—Columbia.—Aspect of the Country on the Road.—Agriculture, &c. &c.

MORGANTON, the principal town of the county of Burke, contains about fifty houses built of wood, and almost all inhabited by tradesmen. One warehouse only, supported by a commercial house at Charleston, is established in this little town, where the inhabitants, for twenty miles round, come and purchase mercery and jewellery goods from England, or give in exchange a part of their produce, which consists chiefly of dried hams, butter, tallow, bear and stag skins, and ginseng, which they bring from the mountains.

From Morganton to Charleston it is computed to be two hundred and eighty-five miles. There are several roads to it, which do not vary in point of distance above twenty miles. Travellers take that where they think of finding the best houses for accommodation: I took the one that leads through Lincolnton, Chester, and Columbia. The distance from Morganton to Lincolnton is forty-five miles. For the whole of this space the soil is extremely bad, and the plantations, straggling five or six miles from each other, have but a middling appearance. The woods are in a great measure composed of different kinds of oaks, and the surface of the ground is covered with grass, intermixed with plants.

Lincolnton, the principal town of the county of Lincoln, is formed by the junction of forty houses, surrounded by the woods like all the small towns of the interior. Two or three large shops, that do the same kind of business as that at Morganton, are established there. The tradesmen who keep them send the produce of their country to Charleston, but they find it sometimes answer their purpose better to stock themselves with goods from Philadelphia, although farther by six hundred miles. Some expedite them by sea to Carolina, whence they go by land to Lincolnton. The freight, a little higher from England to Charleston, and the enormous advance which the merchants lay on their goods, appear the only motives that make them give the preference to those of Philadelphia.

At Lincolnton they print a newspaper in folio, that comes out twice a week. The price of subscription is two dollars per year; but the printer, who is his own editor, takes, by way of payment, for the ease of his country subscribers, flour, rye, wax, &c. at the market price. The advertisements inserted for the inhabitants of the country are generally the surest profit to the printers. The foreign news is extracted from the papers that are published at the sea ports. The federal government, of which the constant aim is to propogate among the people instruction, the knowledge of the laws, grants the editors of periodical papers, throughout the whole extent of the United States, the right to receive, free of postage, the newspapers that they wish to exchange among themselves, or those which are addressed to them.

The county of Lincoln is populated, in a great measure, by Germans from Pennsylvania. Their plantations are kept in the greatest order, and their lands well cultivated. Almost all have negro slaves, and there reigns much more independance among them than in the families of English origin. One may form a correct idea of the industry of some of them by the appearance of the plantation where I stopped, situated upon a branch of the Catabaw River. In eight hundred acres, of which it is composed, a hundred and fifty are cultivated in cotton, Indian corn, wheat, and oats, and dunged annually, which is a great degree of perfection in the present state of the agriculture of this part of the country. Independant of this, he has built in his yard several machines, that the same current of water puts in motion; they consist of a corn mill, a saw mill, another to separate the cotton seeds, a tan-house, a tan-mill, a distillery to make peach brandy, and a small forge, where the inhabitants of the country go to have their horses shod. Seven or eight negro slaves are employed in the different departments, some of which are only occupied at certain periods of the year. Their wives are employed under the direction of the mistress in manufacturing cotton and linen for the use of the family.

The whole of my landlord's taxes, assessed upon his landed property, and these different kinds of industry, did not amount annually to more than seven dollars; whilst under the presidency of J. Adams they had increased to fifty; at the same time his memory is not held in great veneration in Upper Carolina and the Western States, where the political opinion is strongly pronounced in the sense of opposition, and where nobody durst confess himself publicly attached to the federal party.

In all the towns that I travelled through every tanner has his tan mill, which does not cost him above ten dollars to erect. The bark is put into a wooden arch, twelve or fourteen feet in diameter, the edges of which are about fifteen inches high, and it is crushed under the weight of a wheel, about one foot thick, which is turned by a horse, and fixed similar to a cyder-press. For this purpose they generally make use of an old mill-stone, or a wooden wheel, formed by several pieces joined together, and furnished in its circumference with three rows of teeth, also made of wood, about two inches long and twelve or fifteen wide.

From Lincolnton to Chester court house in the state of South Carolina, it is computed to be about seventy miles. For the whole of this space the earth is light and of an inferior quality to that situated between Morganton and Lincolnton, although the mass of the forests is composed of various species of oaks; in the mean time the pines are in such abundance there, that for several miles the ground is covered with nothing else. Plantations are so little increased there, that we scarcely saw twenty where they cultivate cotton or Indian wheat. We passed by several that had been deserted by the owners as not sufficiently productive: for the inhabitants of Georgia and the two Carolinas, who plant nothing but rice, choose frequently rather to make new clearings than to keep their land in a state of producing annually, by regular tillage, as they do in Europe, and even in New England and Pennsylvania. The considerable extent of this country, compared with the trifling population, gives rise to these changes which take place after fifteen or twenty successive harvests.

Chester contains about thirty houses, built of wood; among the number are two inns and two respectable shops. In the principal county towns of the Western and Southern States, they have neither fairs nor markets. The inhabitants sell the produce of their culture to shopkeepers settled in the small towns, or what is more usual in the south, they convey them in waggons to the sea ports.

From Chester the country grows worse in every respect. The traveller no longer meets reception at plantations; he is obliged to put up at inns, where he is badly accommodated both in point of board and lodging, and pays dearer than in any other part of the United States. The reputation of these inns is esteemed according to the quantity and different kinds of spirits that they sell, among which French brandies hold always the first rank, although they are often mixed with water for the third or fourth time.

They reckon fifty-five miles from Chester to Columbia; twenty-five miles on this side we passed through Winesborough, composed of about a hundred and fifty houses. This place is one of the oldest inhabited in Carolina, and several planters of the low country go and spend the summer and autumn there. Fifteen miles on this side Winesborough the *pine barrens* begin, and thence to the sea side the country is one continued forest composed of pines.

Columbia, founded within these twenty years, is the seat of government for the state of South Carolina. It is built about two hundred fathoms from the Catabaw River, upon an uniform spot of ground. The number of its houses does not exceed two hundred; they are almost all built of wood, and painted grey and yellow; and although there are very few of them more than two stories high, they have a very respectable appearance. The legislature, formed by the union of the delegates of different counties that send them in a number proportionate to their population, meet there annually on the first of December, and all the business is transacted in the same month; it then dissolves, and, except at that time, the town derives no particular advantage from being the seat of government.

The inhabitants of the upper country, who do not approve of sending their provisions to Charleston, stop at Columbia, where they dispose of them at several respectable shops established in the town.

The river Catabaw, about twenty fathoms broad, is only navigable during the winter; the rest of the year its navigation is stopped by large rocks that intercept its course. They have been, nevertheless, at work for these several years past in forming a canal to facilitate the descent of the boats, but the work goes on very slowly for the want of hands, although the workmen are paid at the rate of a dollar per day.

Columbia is about a hundred and twenty miles from Charleston; for the whole of this space, and particularly from Orangeburgh, composed of twenty houses, the road crosses an even country, sandy and dry during the summer; whilst in the autumn and winter it is so covered with water that in several places, for the space of eight or ten miles, the horses are up to their middles. Every two or three miles we meet with a miserable log-house upon the road, surrounded with little fields of Indian corn, the slender stalks of which are very seldom more than five or six feet high, and which, from the second harvest, do not yield more than four or five bushels per acre. In the mean time, notwithstanding their sterility, this land is sold at the rate of two dollars per acre.

The extreme unwholesomeness of the climate is

clearly demonstrated by the pale and livid countenances of the inhabitants, who, during the months of September and October, are almost all affected with tertian fevers, insomuch that at this period of the year Georgia and the Lower Carolinas resemble, in some measure, an extensive hospital. Very few persons take any remedy, but wait the approach of the first frosts, which, provided they live so long, generally effect a cure. The negroes are much less subject to intermittent fevers then the whites; and it is seldom that in the great rice plantations there is more than one fifth of them disabled on this account.

CHAP. XXXI.

General observations on the Carolinas and Georgia. —Agriculture and produce peculiar to the upper part of these states.

THE two Carolinas and Georgia are naturally divided into the upper and lower country, but the upper embraces a greater extent. Just at the point where the maritime part is terminated the soil rises gradually till it reaches the Alleghany Mountains, and presents, upon the whole, a ground rather irregular than mountainous, and interspersed with little hills as far as the mountains. The Alleghanies give birth to a great number of creeks or small rivers, the junction of which forms the rivers Pidea Santea,

Savannah, and Alatamaha, which are hardly navigable above two hundred miles from their *embouchure*. In the upper country the most fertile lands are situated upon the borders of these creeks. Those that occupy the intermediate spaces are much less so. The latter are not much cultivated; and even those who occupy them are obliged to be perpetually clearing them, in order to obtain more abundant harvests; in consequence of which a great number of the inhabitants emigrate into the western country, where they are attracted by the extreme fertility of the soil and low price of land; since that of the first class may be purchased for the same money as that of the second in Upper Carolina; and, as we have already said, the latter is scarcely to be compared to that which in Kentucky and Cumberland is ranked in the third.

In the upper country the mass of the forests is chiefly composed of oaks, nut trees, maples, and poplars. Chesnut trees do not begin to appear in these states for sixty miles on this side the mountains. It is only in the remote parts that the inhabitants manufacture maple sugar for their use.

Through the whole of the country the nature of the soil is adapted for the growth of wheat, rye, and Indian corn. Good land produces upward of twenty bushels of Indian wheat per acre, which is commonly worth about half a dollar per bushel. A general consumption is made of it for the support of the inhabitants since, except those who are of German origin, there are very few, as we have before remarked, that make use of wheaten bread. The growth of corn is very circumscribed, and the small quantity of flour that is exported to Charleston and Savannah is sold fifteen per cent. cheaper than that imported from Philadelphia.

The low price to which tobacco is fallen in Europe, within these few years, has made them give up the culture of it in this part of the country. That of green-seed cotton has resumed its place, to the great advantage of the inhabitants, many of whom have since made their fortunes by it. The separation of the seed from the felt that envelopes them is a tedious operation, and which requires many hands, is now simplified by a machine for which the inventor has obtained a patent from the federal government. The legislature of South Carolina paid him, three years since, the sum of a hundred thousand dollars, for all the inhabitants belonging to the state to have the privilege of erecting one. This machine, very simple, and the price of which does not exceed sixty dollars, is put in motion by a horse or by a current of water, and separates from the seed three or four hundred pounds of cotton per day; while by the usual method, a man is not able to separate above thirty pounds. This machine, it is true, has the inconvenience of shortening by haggling it; the wool, on that account, is rather inferior in point of quality, but this inconvenience is, they say, well compensated by the saving of time, and more particularly workmanship.

It is very probable that the various species of fruit trees that we have in France would succeed very well in Upper Carolina. About two hundred miles from the sea-coast the apple trees are magnificent, and in the county of Lincoln several Germans make cyder. But here, as well as in Tennessea, and the greatest part of Kentucky, they cultivate no other but the peach. The other kinds of trees, such as pears, apricots, plumbs, cherries, almonds, mulberries, nuts, and gooseberries, are very little known, except by name. Many of the inhabitants who are independent would be happy to procure some of them, but the distance from the sea-ports renders it very difficult. The major part of the inhabitants do not even cultivate vegetables; and out of twenty there is scarcely one of them that plants a small bed of cabbages; and when they do, it is in the same field as the Indian wheat.

In Upper Carolina the surface of the soil is covered with a kind of grass, which grows in greater abundance as the forests are more open. The woods are also like a common, where the inhabitants turn out their cattle, which they know again by their private mark. Several persons have in their flocks a variety of poll oxen, which are not more esteemed than those of the common species. In the whole course of my travels I never saw any that could be compared to those I have seen in England, which beyond doubt proceeds from the little care that the inhabitants take of them, and from what these animals suffer during the summer, when they are cruelly tormented by an innumerable multitude of ticks and muskitos, and in the winter, through the want of grass, which dries up through the effect of the first frosts. These inconveniencies are still more sensible, during the summer, in the low country, through the extreme heat of the climate. The result is, that the cows give but little milk, and are dry at the end of three or four months. In the environs of Philadelphia and New York, where they bestow the same care upon them as in England, they are, on the contrary, as fine, and give as great a quantity of milk.

The horses that they rear in this part of the

southern states are inferior to those of the western. The inhabitants keep but very few sheep, and those who have a dozen are accounted to have a great number.

The commercial intercourse of the Upper Carolines and Georgia is carried on, in a great measure, with Charleston, which is not much farther than Wilmington and Savannah. The inhabitants go there in preference, because the commerce is more active, and the sales more easy. The articles they carry there consists chiefly in short cotton, tobacco, hams, salt butter, wax, stag, and bear skins, and cattle. They take, in return, coarse iron ware, tea, coffee, powder sugar, coarse cloths, and fine linen, but no bar iron, the upper country abounding in mines of that metal, and those which are worked sufficing the wants of the inhabitants. They also bring salt from the sea-ports, since there are no salt pits in any part of the Atlantic states. The carriage of these goods is made in large waggons with four wheels, drawn by four or six horses, that travel about twenty-four miles a day, and encamp every evening in the woods. The price of conveyance is about three shillings and four-pence per hundred weight for every hundred miles.

Although the climate of the Upper Carolinas is infinitely more wholesome than that of the lower parts, it is not, in the mean time, at two hundred miles, and even two hundred and fifty, from the ocean, that a person is safe from the yellow fever.

Eight-tenths of the inhabitants of this part of the country are in the same situation as those of Tennessea and Kentucky. They reside, like the latter, in log-houses isolated in the woods, which are left open in the night as well as the day. They live in the same manner with regard to their domestic affairs, and follow the same plans of agriculture. Notwithstanding there are many of them whose moral characters, perhaps, are not so unspotted as those of the western inhabitants, it is probably altered by associating with the Scotch and Irish who come every year in great numbers to settle in the country, and who teach them a part of their vices and defects, the usual attendants on a great population. The major part of these new adventurers go into the upper country, where they engage to serve, for a year or two, those persons who have paid the captain of the ship for their passage.

CHAP. XXXII.

Low part of the Carolines and Georgia.—Agriculture.—Population.—Arrival at Charleston.

THE low country of the two Carolinas extends from the borders of the sea for a hundred and twenty or a hundred and fifty miles, widening as it gets towards the south. The space that this extent embraces presents an even and regular soil, formed by a blackish sand, rather deep in parts, in which there are neither stones nor flints; in consequence of which they seldom shoe their horses in that part of the United States. Seven-tenths of the country are covered with pines of one species, or *pinus palustris*, which, as the soil is drier and lighter, grow loftier and not so branchy. These trees, frequently twenty feet distant from each other, are not damaged by the fire that they make here annually in the woods, at the commencement of spring, to burn the grass and other plants that the frost has killed. These pines, encumbered with very few branches, and which split even, are preferred to other trees to form fences for plantations. Notwithstanding the sterility of the land where they grow, they are sometimes interspersed with three kinds of oaks; viz. the *quercus nigra*; the *quercus catasbœi*, and the *quercus obtusiloba*. The wood of the two first is only fit to burn, whilst that of the other is of an excellent use, as I have before remarked.

The Pine Barrens are crossed by little swamps, in the midst of which generally flows a rivulet. These swamps, from ten to forty fathoms broad, are sometimes more than a mile in length, and border on others, more spacious and marshy, near the rivers.

Each have different degrees of fertility, clearly indicated by the trees that grow there exclusively, and which are not to be found in the upper country. Thus the chesnut oak, or *quercus prinus palustris*, the *magnolia grandiflora*, the *magnolia tripetala*, the *nyssa biflora*, &c. flourish only in swamps where the soil is of a good quality, and continually cool, moist, and shady. In some parts of these same swamps, that are half the year submerged, where the earth is black, muddy, and reposes upon a clayey bottom, the acacia-leaved cypress, the *gleditsia monosperme*, the lyric oak, and the bunchy nut-tree, the nuts of which are small, and break easily between the fingers. The aquatic oak, the red maple, the *magnolia glauca*, the *liquidambar stiracyflua*, the *nyssa villosa*, the *Gordonia lasyanthus*, and the *laurus Caroliniensis*, cover, on the contrary, exclusively the narrow swamps of the Pine Barrens.

The Spanish beard, *tillandsia asneoides*, a kind of moss of a greyish colour, which is several feet in length, and which grows in abundance upon the oaks and other trees, is again a plant peculiar to the low country.

In those districts where there are no pines, the soil is not so dry, deeper, and more productive. We found there white oaks, or *quercus alba*, aquatic oaks, or *quercus aquatica*, chesnut oaks, or *quercus prinus palustris*, and several species of nut-trees. The whole of these trees are here an index of the greatest fertility, which does not take place in the western country, as I have before observed.

The best rice plantations are established in the great swamps, that favour the watering of them when convenient. The harvests are abundant there, and the rice that proceeds from them, stripped of its husk, is larger, more transparent, and is sold dearer than that which is in a drier soil, where they have not the means or facility of irrigation. The culture of rice in the southern and maritime part of the United States has greatly diminished within these few years; it has been in a great measure replaced by that of cotton, which affords greater profit to the planters, since they compute a good cotton harvest equivalent to two of rice. The result is, that many rice fields have been transformed into those of cotton, avoiding as much as possible the water penetrating.

The soil most adapted for the culture of cotton is in the isles situate upon the coast. Those which belong to the state of Georgia produce the best of cotton, which is known in the French trade by the name of Georgia cotton, fine wool, and in England by that of Sea Island cotton. The seed of this kind of cotton is of a deep black, and the wool fine and very long. In February 1803 it was sold at Charleston at 1s. 8d. per pound, whilst that which grows in the upper country is not worth above seventeen or eighteen pence. The first is exported to England, and the other goes to France; but what is very remarkable is, that whenever by any circumstance they import these two qualities into our ports, they only admit of a difference of from twelve to fifteen per cent. The cotton planters have particularly to dread the frosts that set in very early, and that frequently do great damage to the crops by freezing one half of the stalks, so that the cotton has not an opportunity to ripen.

In all the plantations they cultivate Indian corn. The best land brings from fifteen to twenty bushels. They plant it, as well as the cotton, about two feet and a half distance, in parallel furrows from fifteen to eighteen inches high. The seed of this kind of Indian corn is round, and very white. When boiled it is preferable to that cultivated in the middle and western states, and in Upper Carolina. The chief part of what they grow is destined to support the negroes nine months in the year; their allowance is about two pounds per day, which they boil in water after having pounded it a little; the other three months they are fed upon yams. They never give them meat. In the other parts of the United States they are better treated, and live nearly upon the same as their masters, without having any set allowance. Indian corn is sold at Charleston for ten shillings per bushel, about fifty-five pounds weight.

Thus rice, long cotton, yams, and Indian wheat, are the only cultures in the maritime part of the southern states; the temperature of the climate, and the nature of the soil, which is too light or too moist, being in no wise favourable for that of wheat or any kind of grain.

Through the whole of the low country the agricultural labours are performed by negro slaves, and the major part of the planters employ them to drag the plough; they conceive the land is better cultivated, and calculate besides that in the course of a year a horse, for food and looking after, costs ten times more than a negro, the annual expense of which does not exceed fifteen dollars.

I shall abstain from any reflexion concerning this, as the opinion of many people is fixed.

The climate of Lower Carolina and Georgia is too warm in summer to be favourable to European fruit-trees, and too cold in winter to suit those of the Caribbees. The fig is the only tree that succeeds tolerably well; again, the figs turn sour a few days after they have acquired the last degree of maturity, which must doubtless be attributed to the constant dampness of the atmosphere.

In the environs of Charleston, and in the isles that border the coast, the orange-trees stand the winter in the open fields, and are seldom damaged by the frosts; but at ten miles distance, in the interior, they freeze every year even with the ground, although those parts of the country are situate under a more southerly latitude than Malta and Tunis. The oranges that they gather in Carolina are not good to eat. Those consumed there come from the island of St. Anastasia, situate opposite St. Augustin, the capital of East Florida; they are sweet, very large, fine skinned, and more esteemed than those brought from the Carribbees. About fifty years ago the seeds were brought from India, and given to an inhabitant of this island, who has so increased them that he has got an orchard of forty acres. I had an opportunity of seeing this beautiful plantation when I was at Florida in 1788.

In the general verification of the United States, published in 1800, the popul tion of North Carolina, comprising negro slaves, amounted to four hundred and seventy-eight thousand inhabitants, that of Georgia to one hundred and sixty-three thousand, and that of South Carolina to three hundred and forty-six thousand. Not having been able to see the private extracts of the two former states, I am unacquainted with the proportion that there is between the whites and blacks, and the difference that exists between the population of the low and high countries; however an idea may be formed by the verification of South Carolina, where they reckon in the low country, comprising the town of Charleston, thirty-six thousand whites and a hundred thousand negroes, and in the high country one hundred and sixty-three thousand whites and forty-six thousand negroes.

I arrived at Charleston on the 18th of October 1802, three months and a half after my departure from Philadelphia, having travelled over a space of nearly eighteen hundred miles. I staid at Carolina till the 1st of March 1803, the epoch when I embarked for France on board the same ship that had taken me to America eighteen months before, and arrived at Bourdeaux on the 26th of March 1803.

THE END.

SHURY, PRINTER.

WS - #0138 - 271223 - C0 - 229/152/18 - PB - 9780461996401 - Gloss Lamination